Norfolk, The Wash and Humber
Lowestoft to Spurn Head

Peter Harvey

Published by
FB Imray Laurie Norie & Wilson GmbH
Ölzeltgasse 3/10, 1030 Vienna, Austria
☎ +43 1 869 90 90
Email sales@imray.com
www.imray.com
2022 (Reprinted 2026)

All rights reserved. No part of this publication may be reproduced, transmitted or used in any form by any means – graphic, electronic or mechanical, including photocopying, recording, taping or information storage and retrieval systems or otherwise – without the prior permission of the Publishers.

First edition 2022 (Reprinted 2026)

© Text: Peter Harvey 2022
Peter Harvey has asserted his rights to be identified as the author of this work in accordance with the Copyright, Designs and Patents Act 1988.

© Plans: Imray Laurie Norie & Wilson Ltd 2022

© Photographs: Peter Harvey unless otherwise credited

ISBN 978 178679 147 4

CAUTION
While every effort has been taken to ensure accuracy, neither the publishers nor the author will hold themselves responsible for errors, omissions or alterations in this publication. They will at all times be grateful to receive information which tends to the improvement of the work.

SUPPLEMENTS AND UPDATES
This pilot book will be amended at intervals by the issue of correctional supplements. These are published at www.imray.com and may be downloaded free of charge. Printed copies are also available on request from the publishers at the above address.

British Library Cataloguing in Publication Data.
A catalogue record for this book is available from the British Library.

PLANS
The plans in this guide are not to be used for navigation. They are designed to support the text and should at all times be used with up to date navigational charts.

This product has been derived in part from material obtained from the UK Hydrographic Office with the permission of the UK Hydrographic Office, Her Majesty's Stationery Office.

© British Crown Copyright, 2022. All rights reserved.

Licence number GB AA - 005 - Imrays

THIS PRODUCT IS NOT TO BE USED FOR NAVIGATION

NOTICE: The UK Hydrographic Office (UKHO) and its licensors make no warranties or representations, express or implied, with respect to this product. The UKHO and its licensors have not verified the information within this product or quality assured it.

This work has been corrected to May 2022.

Printed in the United Kingdom by Halstan & Co. Ltd

CONTENTS

PREFACE	**v**
Acknowledgements	vi
Author bio	vi
INTRODUCTION	**1**
Cruising information	2
Tidal Streams	3
Symbols used on plan	6
Recommended charts	6
Abbreviations	7
COASTAL PASSAGES	**9**
NORTH NORFOLK	**15**
Blakeney	17
Wells-next-the-Sea	20
Burnham Overy Harbour	23
Brancaster Staithe	26
Thornham	29
THE WASH	**31**
King's Lynn	34
The River Nene to Sutton Bridge & Wisbech	40
Cross Keys Marina, Sutton Bridge	42
Wisbech	44
Fosdyke and Boston	47
Fosdyke	49
Boston	51
Wainfleet Haven	54
THE HUMBER	**59**
Saltfleet	61
Tetney	61
Grimsby	63
Stone Creek	66
Skitter Haven	67
Hedon	68
Hull	68
New Holland	72
Barrow-upon-Humber	72
Barton-upon-Humber	74
Hessle	76
Ferriby Sluice and South Ferriby	77
Winteringham Haven	81
Brough	83
Broomfleet	85
Above Apex Light	87
The River Trent to Gainsborough	87
The River Ouse to Goole	88
Goole	90
INDEX	**92**

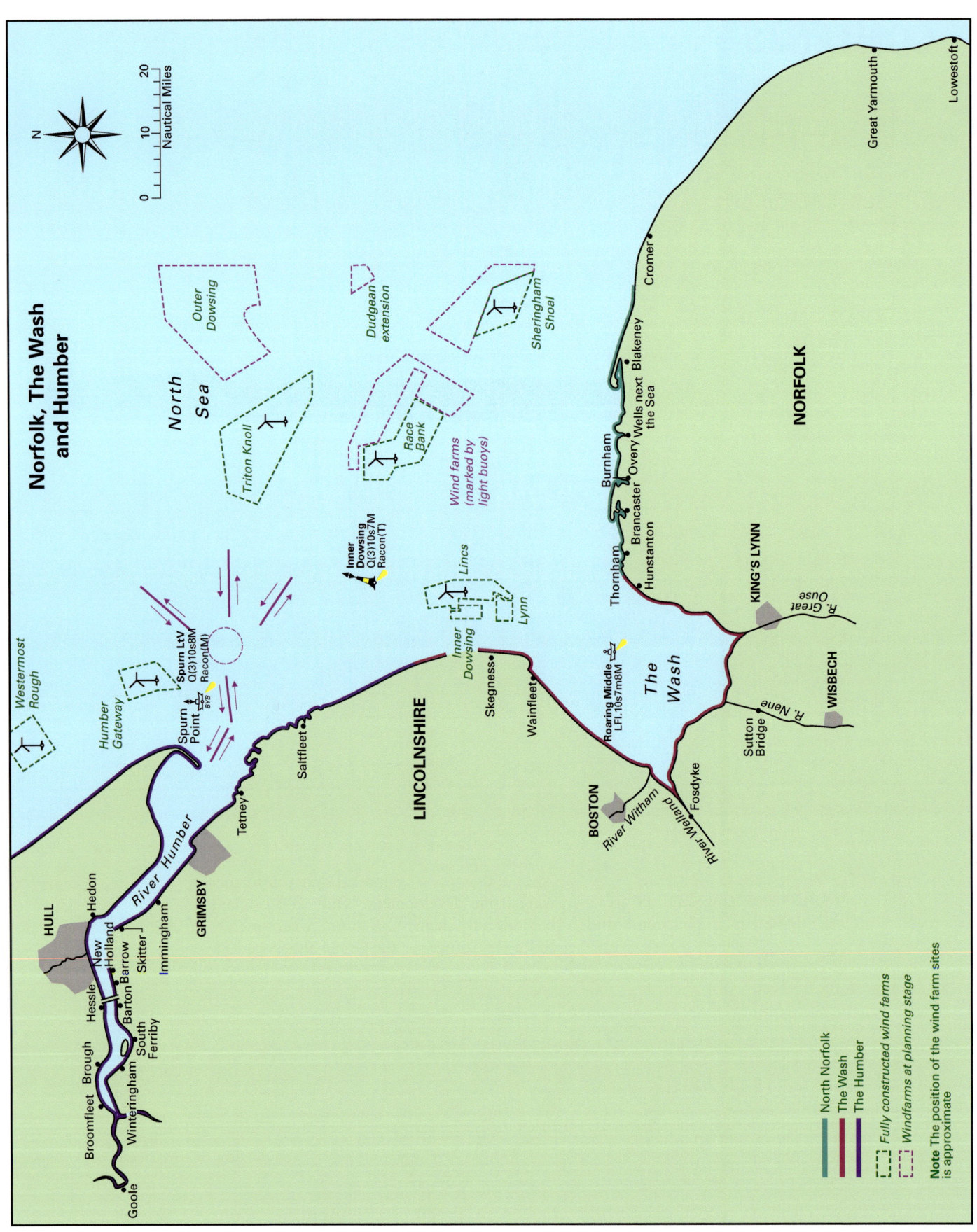

The Wash. Where the sun sets over the sea on the east coast
Gary Garford

PREFACE

This new title is a direct descendant of *Tidal Havens of The Wash and Humber*, ably created and maintained by Henry Irving between 1976 and 2011. It was a privilege to inherit Henry's work and I hope that I have retained his enthusiasm for this unique cruising area. Much has changed in the region since the 6th edition of 2011. More recently, despite the pandemic, mooring facilities have been enlarged in at least two of The Wash ports. And while the boating scene may not be as vibrant as in more popular locations, in comparison with 1976 – or even 1996, there has been a revolution!

Of greatest interest will be the growth of available moorings and, as an extension of that, the improvement of the region as somewhere to enjoy leisure time afloat.

But some things never change and the area's tidal nature is one. All ports, harbours and havens are tidally constrained to some degree which brings a different dimension to day sailing. However, a preparedness to anchor opens up some idyllic destinations and part of this edition is devoted to the identification of such hideaways.

North Norfolk's tidal creeks and havens, save for channel changes, are much as ever, except ashore where populations are significantly increased during summer months, compounded by the recent 'staycation' effect. Wells-next-the-Sea, with a static population of 2,000 or so, always swelled to 12,000 in holiday times, but even the Blakeneys and Burnhams of this world have been catching up in visitor numbers. Hardly a Sunday travel supplement goes by without North Norfolk featuring and it seems to have been working.

In The Wash, destinations are now numerous, at least relative to 2011. Fosdyke Yacht Haven has more than doubled in size and the range of marine trades on hand is considerable. The boatyard in Wisbech thrives too and available trades there have increased. Sutton Bridge, nearer the mouth of the River Nene and below the swing bridge, boasts modern, fully serviced pontoons and, of all The Wash ports, can be reached even when a northerly blow excludes others. King's Lynn too has a fully serviced pontoon, functioning as a town quay. Immediately adjacent to the old town, this is popular with visitors from seaward and inland alike and is proving the catalyst for further waterfront development. Only Boston lags behind, but schemes are afoot. Meantime the River Witham above the Grand Sluice sea lock continues to provide a destination for those not constrained by air draught.

In Grimsby, the Humber Cruising Association continues to provide a welcome and the pontoons and shoreside facilities there are more in demand than ever. Navigationally, the use of Grimsby by wind farm service vessels has resulted in a recommended route to and from the south, avoiding the buoyed, deep-water channel and the separation zone. This is shown on all current charts and should be the preferred route for all small craft.

Hull Marina is now part of the Aquavista Group owning eighteen coastal and inland marinas in many parts of the country. Hull itself benefitted greatly from being designated UK City of Culture 2017 and continues to grow in stature and identity. The marina and its environs are more than worthy of an extended stay.

The smaller havens, remain an option for shoal draught vessels which can take the ground, and the various yacht and boat clubs are invariably active and welcoming. Channels constantly change, however, and local knowledge should always be sought as charts showing this detail can be quickly out of date.

But what else is different since 2011? The onward march of offshore windfarms has continued here with the Lincs and Race Bank arrays adding their footprint to those of Lynn and Inner Dowsing. From the deck of a small boat these all appear contiguous off the northwest corner of The Wash, and only Sheringham Shoal further east stands out separately. That planned for Docking Shoal was cancelled in 2015 for want of the necessary permissions, the natural environment having won that round. Whatever one's opinion of their worth, they do represent a valuable visual aid to navigation, not only by virtue of their scale but their development has added considerably to local buoyage.

The regional marine tourism scheme Sail The Wash www.sailthewash.com has been instrumental in presenting the area in a more user-friendly light and is aimed at the waterborne visitor. It remains that no matter how crowded a promenade, viewed from one's own deck a little way offshore makes for a wholly different perspective.

Peter Harvey
2022

Acknowledgements

Gathering information, correct at the time of writing for this new title, was not achieved without the help of others to whom I am indebted. To Ian Newton; for some north Norfolk insights, and to Bob Cowley of the Humber Mouth Yacht Club for invaluable local knowledge. For north Lincolnshire information in general, Sam Brockett; and in Goole, Laird Cremer-Evans. In Hull, Graham Richardson at Hull Marina and Mike Abbey of ABP Humber. In Grimsby, Tom Poulsen of the Humber Cruising Association and Simon Winship, the Grimsby and Cleethorpes YC.

For Blakeney and Morston, Charlie Ward and Mike Mirams and for some Humber gems, which would otherwise have been lost, the written works of the late Rodney Clapson. For The Wash, all the ever-helpful harbour masters and Andy Foster, marina manager on the River Nene. To my long-suffering shipmates, Robin Hooper and Sean Finlay, my thanks for their companionship afloat and to my wife Catherine for continuing to cope with the vagaries of sailing plans. More recently, a perspective, and some photographs, from Mark Ashley-Miller, who is circumnavigating the UK and Ireland in support of the charity Seafarers UK, have been invaluable. Finally, an appreciation to Gary Garford for his keen photographic eye which has added greatly to my attempts to convey the appeal of this fascinating coast.

With thanks to Anje Valk, author of Vaarwijzer, De Engelse oostkust. Ramsgate tot de Schotse Grens for her encouragement and for talking my publication up in The Netherlands even before it was finished!

Author bio

An east coast devotee, Peter Harvey began his sailing at school with the building of a Heron dinghy. Racing small boats on the River Blackwater followed, before work life meant service at sea and ashore with both navies. Cruising under sail has included several seasons beyond the Arctic circle, in the Mediterranean, the Baltic, Western Australia and a memorable Tall Ships Race. His full-time career culminated as Harbourmaster for one of The Wash ports. Now semi-retired, he applies himself to marine development projects with the accent on the leisure boating market. He sails a Trintella 38, which with 1.9m draught would not be readily considered the ideal Norfolk, Wash and Humber boat, but it just goes to show how wrong people can be about this unique part of the world.

Dedication

Both author and publisher are indebted to Henry Irving for handing on his *Tidal Havens of The Wash and Humber* from which this new title is derived. For more than 40 years, visiting sailors were encouraged by Henry's explorations of the varied creeks and expanses of this region, and to this day he remains an enthusiastic proponent of this corner of the east coast.

INTRODUCTION

'A harbour, even if it is a little harbour, is a good thing, since adventurers come into it as well as go out and the life in it grows strong, because it takes something from the world and has something to give in return.'
Sarah Orne Jewett. American novelist and poet. *Country By-Ways* (1881)

This pilot covers a part of the UK east coast which, arguably, has the least leisure boating activity by region. And yet it has much to offer the coastal visitor. Its light has been hidden under a bushel for too long. Time then for change. Time for those who enjoy their leisure afloat to look to new and bigger horizons. Plenty of those around here!

The North Sea coasting corridor, picking its way through many sands, knolls and ridges has served for centuries. James Cook passed this way. And in the second world war, from the likes of Great Yarmouth and Grimsby, trawlers went to war to keep the inshore convoy routes clear. All their stories are still proudly told locally.

Other parts of the country can be enjoyed with short passages and little tidal constraint at origin or destination. Not so here. But this stretch of coast between Lowestoft and Spurn Head can be sailed to advantage. With a willingness to anchor, either for the tranquillity that comes only from a night on the hook or to wait awhile for a favourable tide, new opportunities abound.

By leaving the boat for a day or two and venturing ashore by other means, the region's history, including its rich maritime heritage, is there for the asking. Public transport options in this pursuit are frequent, plentiful and in some cases attractively quirky. What though is on offer to the enquiring sailor? A few examples by way of flavour:

From Great Yarmouth, and indeed Lowestoft, there is access to over a hundred miles of inshore cruising on tidal rivers, lakes and meres, with but one lock and a landscape as much like the Netherlands as Holland is itself. The Norfolk Broads, the result of peat diggings which flooded in the fourteenth century, are now a national park and Britain's largest protected wetland. A tapestry of recreational water and wildlife, the Broads are often overlooked as an option for the cruising sailor from seaward and while beyond the scope of this pilot, not to raise awareness of this possibility would be an omission.
www.mynorfolkbroadsboating.co.uk

Coasting north from Lowestoft and very soon, Cromer appears with its lighthouse and pleasure pier. Little chance of mooring off for a run ashore but why miss it? Famous for its locally caught crabs and lobsters, its beach-launched fishing boats work much as they always have. And possibly its most famous son, Henry Blogg, still the most decorated RNLI coxswain has, justifiably, a museum here to his name. Given an idle moment, find a copy of *The Loss of the English Trader* by Cyril Jolly and marvel.

How though to follow this trail? One way is by leaving the boat in Lowestoft, taking a bus to the cathedral city of Norwich with, perhaps, an overnight stay, then the train through the rising countryside to Cromer. Maybe a side trip to nearby Sheringham and the heritage railway line along the coast.

Or from Cromer, the North Norfolk coastal bus service takes in the pretty tidal harbours which might not otherwise be possible for the deeper draughted yacht.

The Humber too offers much more of interest ashore than in the immediate vicinity of the two main marinas, Grimsby and Hull. Both banks of the estuary are well served with public transport, especially rail and, again, if deep draught prevents direct visits to the many tidal havens, this needn't preclude following a fascinating, local maritime trail.

John Harrison, the man who changed the world through his clockmaking skills, worked his magic in Barrow-upon-Humber, and fine, traditional boatbuilding is still practised in Barton-upon-Humber, itself an historic local centre of marine industry.

Brough, west of Hull is where, as early as 1916, the seaplane was developed, and more recently where the Blackburn Buccaneer, the Fleet Air Arm carrier strike aircraft, was built. Later still, Harrier jump jets were built there under the BAE Systems banner.

On a more prosaic level, two Michelin starred restaurants can be found on the south shore. And not to forget Grimsby and Hull whose seafaring histories are rich stories in their own rights, well told within a biscuit toss of where you'd moor up.

Finally, no visit to the Humber would be complete without an anchor stop inside the Spurn, a call at the only full-time professionally manned RNLI station and a farewell drink at the Crown and Anchor in Kilnsea.

Many of the settlements which front these coasts and rivers are reviving their links with the sea and reaping the benefits, socially and economically.

Over the last twenty years, and certainly in the period since the 6th edition of this pilot, The Wash in particular, in its 'offer' to the leisure boating market, has changed beyond all recognition and continues to evolve. While not yet complete, what's now available provides ready links in to a unique, even magical marine environment. This region is a place for the small boat sailor who is looking for a cruising ground with a difference to discover. Best not risk wishing you'd found it sooner.

The Norfolk coast path is an ideal way to see this coast

Launched, at last!
Catherine Harvey

Cruising information

Coastguard

Station	MMSI	Telephone
Humber	002320007	+44 1262 672317

National Coastwatch Institution

The NCI is a voluntary organisation set up to provide a visual watch along the shores of England and Wales. They will respond to vessels requesting radio checks, local weather, sea state conditions, relevant inshore waters forecast and information on a range of local facilities. Call on VHF 65 using appropriate call sign eg *Exmouth NCI*. For details see www.nci.org.uk ☎ +44 1579 347392

Station	Telephone	Approx position	Latitude	Longitude
Felixstowe	01394 670808	Martello Tr P	51°56'·9N	1°20'·1E
Gorleston	01493 440384	S of Gt Yarmouth	52°34'·3N	1°44'·3E
Caister	07257 977613	Beach	52°38'·7N	1°44'·2E
Mundesley	01263 722399	Cliff top	52°52'·7N	1°26'·4E
Runton	01263 513725	Top of beach	52°56'·2N	1°16'·5E
Wells	01328 710587	W of river ent	52°58'·4N	0°51'·1E
Skegness	01754 610884		53°10'·0N	0°21'·1E

Regional winds

The principal characteristic of winds in this region is great variability, both from the depressions which cross the area and the topography of the UK east coast. Winds between S through W to NW are most common in all seasons, but from spring there is an increase in winds from N and E. The quietest period is May to August when Force 7 and above are experienced on less than 1 to 3 days per month. Sea breezes from around noon are typical from spring to early autumn. For the most part, expect SW then NE in terms of likelihood.

Storm surges

With much of the region low lying, tidal flooding has long since been a major risk. And even now, despite decades of augmented flood protection measures, the risk remains. This is particularly so when big spring tides coincide with N or NE gales, resulting in a tidal surge along the entire east coast and the North Sea in general. Of significance to small boat sailors in these shoal waters is the scope for tides either exceeding or not meeting prediction. This is due to contrary winds and/or atmospheric pressure. https://ntslf.org/storm-surges/surge-forecast is a useful source of real time observations relative to prediction.

The shipping forecast

Radio 4 LW, 198kHz, at 0048*, 0520*, 1201,1754 LT (*also VHF and MW.) Areas and terms used are described below.

Inshore Waters forecasts

Follow the 0048 and 0520 shipping forecasts on Radio 4.

Actual reports

The 0520 forecast is followed by reports of actual weather from coastal stations and light vessels. Reports are from locations shown on the UK sea area chartlet. Some of the stations are automatic and measure visibility but not 'weather' ie there are no reports of rain, drizzle, showers, etc. The 0048 forecast is followed by an extended list of stations.

Some coastal reports are broadcast on NAVTEX 490kHz.

Maritime Safety Information (MSI) broadcasts

The Maritime and Coastguard Agency states that NAVTEX is the primary means for broadcasting MSI but many leisure sailors use marine VHF, public service radio, harbour notice boards and, increasingly, the internet.

UK Inshore Waters Forecasts and MSI on VHF

After an initial announcement on VHF 16 it is then transmitted on one of VHF 62, 63 or 64.

Coastguard Operation Centre (CGOC) & Area	Humber (Berwick to Southwold)	
Inshore Forecast Area 24 hour forecast, 24 hour outlook. Valid up to 12M offshore	Berwick to Whitby, Whitby to Gibraltar Point. Gibraltar Point to N Foreland	
Shipping Forecast Areas	Tyne, Dogger, Fisher, Humber, German Bight, Thames	
Broadcast times LT and schedules	B	0130 1330
	C	0430 1630
	A	1730 1930
	C	1030 2230

Schedule A
Full maritime safety information broadcast, including new inshore forecast and outlook, gale warnings, general synopsis and shipping forecast for appropriate sea areas, WZ navigation warnings, SUBFACTS and GUNFACTS where appropriate, three-day fisherman's forecast (October to March).

Schedule B
New inshore forecast, new outlook, gale warnings.

Schedule C
Repetition of inshore forecast and gale warnings as per previous Schedule A or B broadcast plus new strong wind warning.

Tidal Streams

The Admiralty Tidal Stream atlas *NP252 North Sea, Southern Portion* is not only at too small a scale to be useful in this cruising ground, but it under reports the strengths of the streams, in some instances to a dangerous extent. It has been thought advisable, therefore, to construct a tidal stream series for the area, based on the most appropriate and strategic tidal diamonds of all the local large scale Admiralty charts. The selection of a time datum presented a problem. Most atlases refer to HW Dover; most local tide tables, even as far afield as Wells and Blakeney, are based on Hull Fish Dock. It was decided to use the latter, on the grounds that these times are those which the cruising sailor is most likely to have to hand. Moreover, Hull is a convenient round five hours before HW Dover, so it does not require Einsteinian mathematical skills to make the conversion.

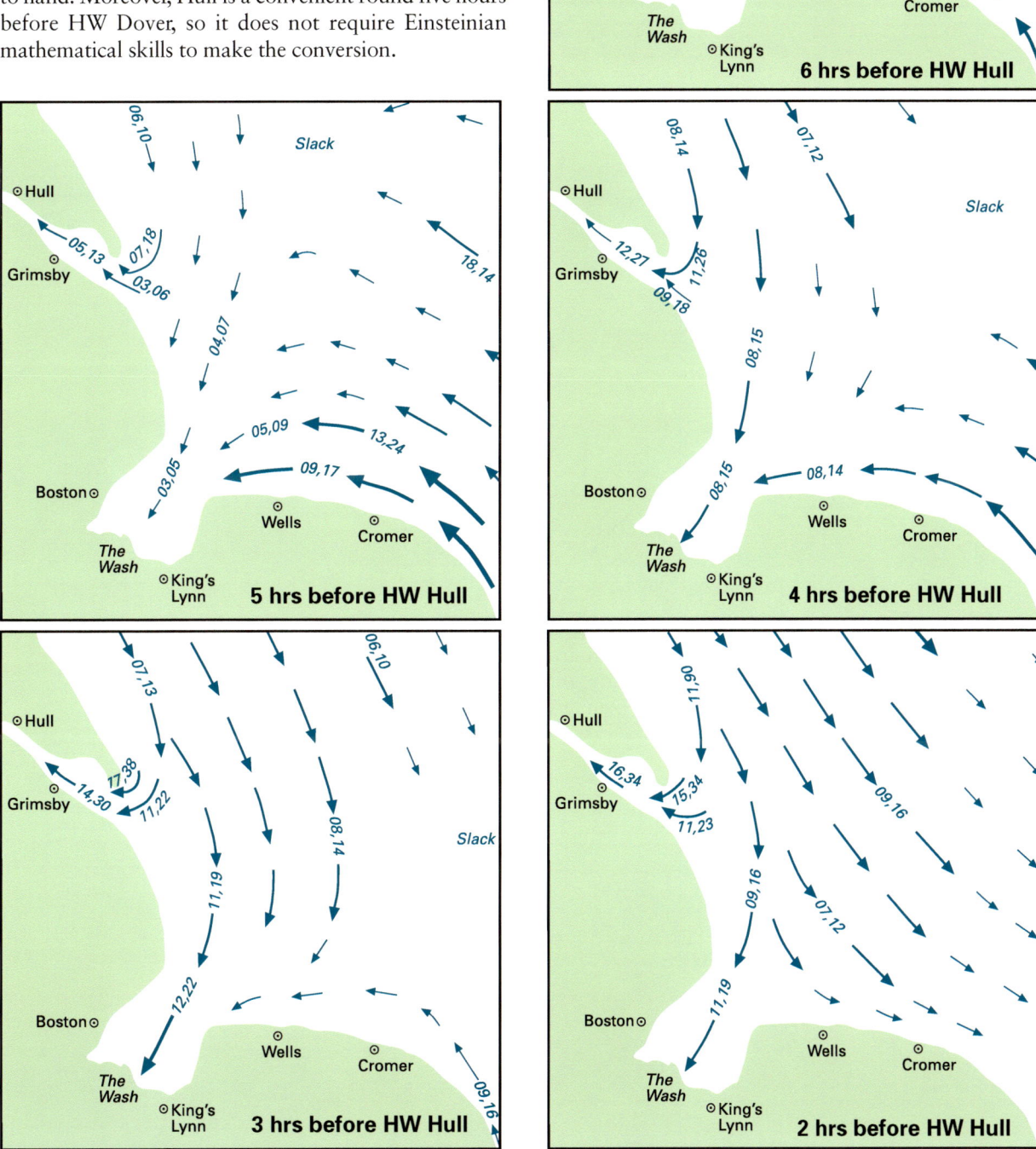

The figures against the arrows denote mean rates in tenths of a knot at neaps and spring. Thus 06, 11 indicates a mean neap rate of 0·6 knots and a mean spring rate of 1·1 knots.

Norfolk, The Wash and Humber

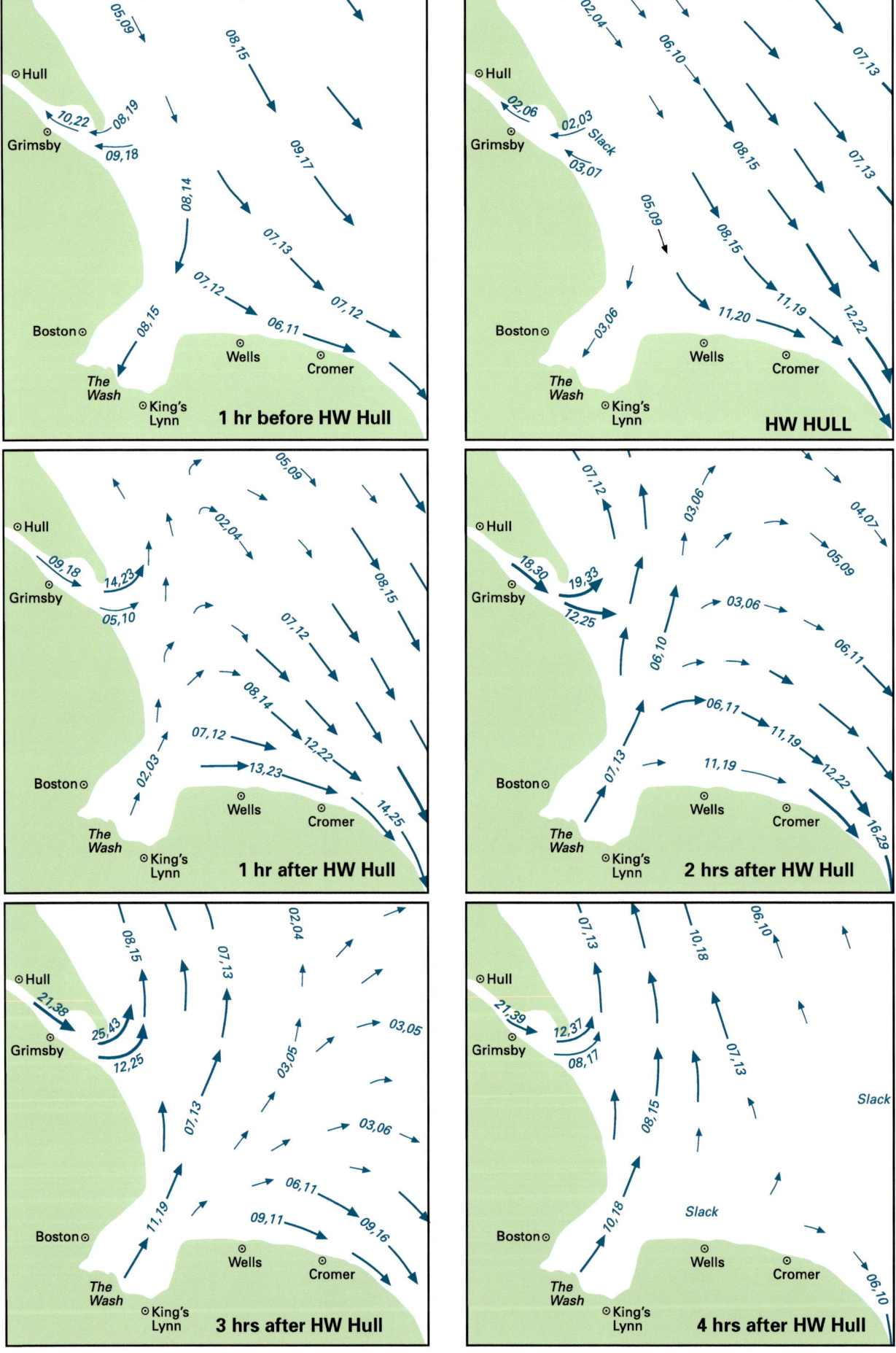

Tidal Streams

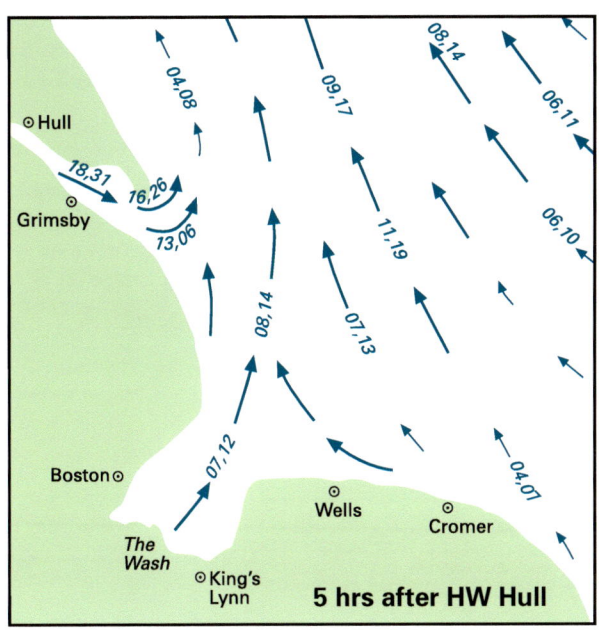

5 hrs after HW Hull

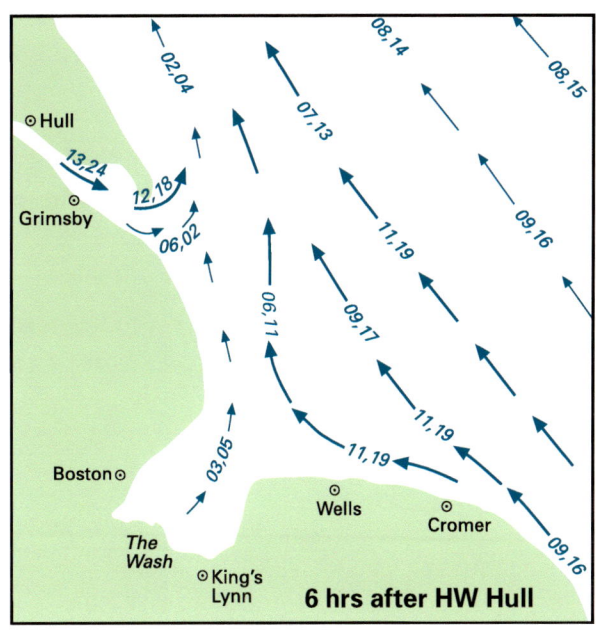

6 hrs after HW Hull

Distances and tidal information
Distance and tidal difference from Hull (Fish Dock)

	Distances in sea miles	Tidal differences (add to or subtract from HW Hull)		Rise of tide at selected points	
				Springs	Neaps
Hull (Fish Dock)	0.0			6·8m (22·3ft)	3·4m (11·2ft)
New Holland	2·0				
Barrow-upon-Humber	3·0	+0008(S)	+0015(N)	7·0m (23·0ft)	3·0m (9·8ft)
Barton-upon-Humber	4·5				
Hessle	3·7				
Ferriby Sluice	7·6	+0012(S)	+0025(N)	6·7m (22·0ft)	3·0m (9·8ft)
Brough (via Read's I.)	11·5	+0019(S)	+0034(N)	6·7m (22·0ft)	3·4m (11·2ft)
Trent Falls	15·0	+0030(S)	+0050(N)	5·5m (18·1ft)	3·2m (10·5ft)
Goole	24·0	+0105(S)	+0120(N)	5·5m (18·1ft)	2·7m (8·9ft)
Keadby	24·5	+0100(S)	+0125(N)	4·5m (14·8ft)	2·8m (9·2ft)
Hedon Haven	3·8	−0010m		6·6m (21·7ft)	3·3m (10·8ft)
N. Killingholme	6·8	−0023(S)	−0018(N)	6·4m (21·0ft)	3·2m (10·5ft)
Grimsby (via Burcom Flats)	14·0	−0040(S)	−0030(N)	6·0m (19·7ft)	3·0m (9·8ft)
Haile Sand Fort (Tetney)	19·0	−0050		5·8m (19·0ft)	2·8m (9·2ft)
Haile Sand Buoy	24·0	−0100			
Saltfleet	31·0	−0050			
Wainfleet	54·0	Same			
Boston (via Wainfleet)	72·0	+0011		6·7m (22·0ft)	3·0m (9·8ft)
Fosdyke (via Wainfleet)	73·0	+0015			
Sutton Bridge	74·0	+0008			
Wisbech	81·5	+0018			
Dog-in-a-Doublet Sluice	95·6	+0143			
Lynn	74·0	+0015		6·8m (22·3ft)	3·0m (9·8ft)
Denver Sluice	88·0	+0115		3·0m (9·8ft)	1·7m (5·6ft)
Burnham Flats Buoy	51·6	−0008		6·0m (19·7ft)	2·8m (9·2ft)
Brancaster Bar	62·1	Same		5·8m (19·0ft)	3·1m (10·2ft)
Burnham Harbour Mouth	62·6	Same		5·5m (18·1ft)	3·0m (9·8ft)
Wells Fairway Buoy	63·4	Same		5·3m (17·4ft)	2·9m (9·5ft)
Wells Quay	65·5	+0035			
Blakeney Wreck Buoy	67·5	+0008		5·0m (16·4ft)	2·6m (8·5ft)
Blakeney Pit	69·5	+0030			

Norfolk, The Wash and Humber

Symbols used on plans

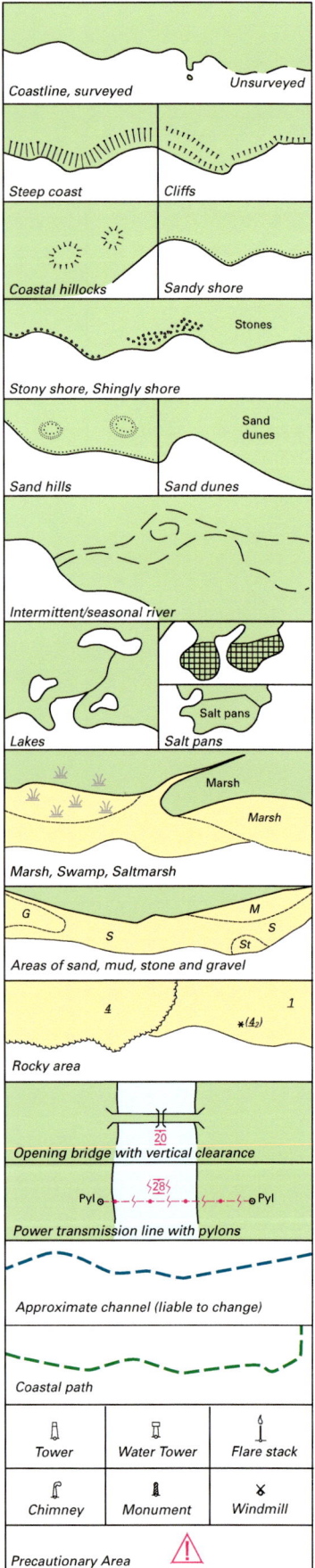
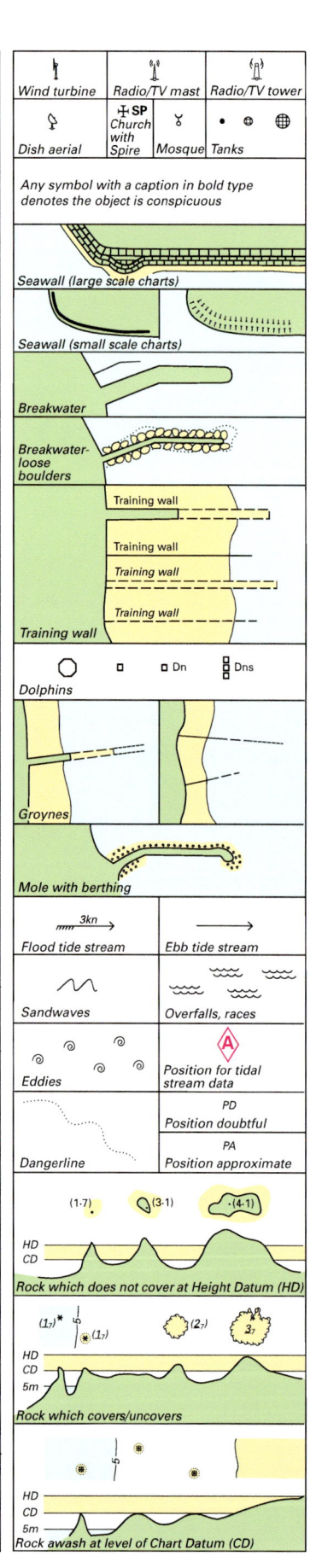
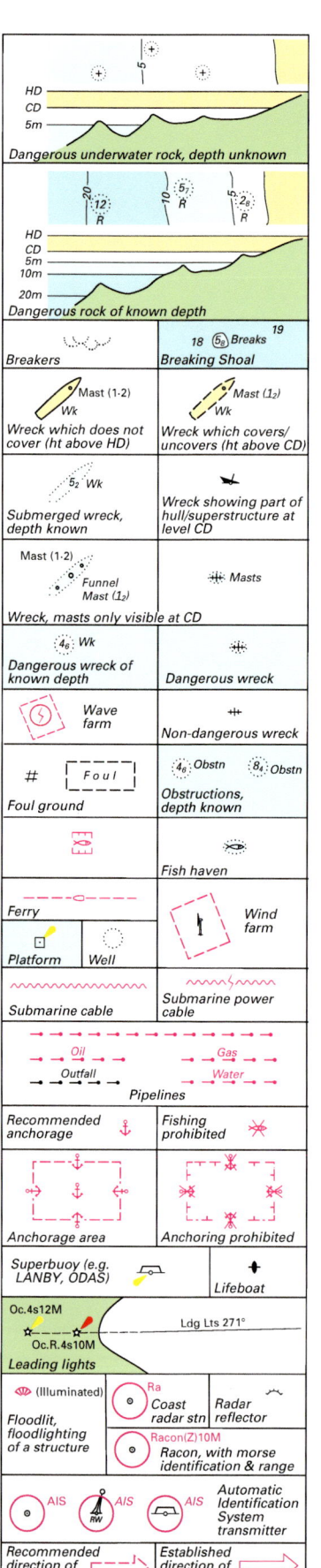

Recommended charts

Imray

Y9	The Wash
C28	East Coast Harwich to Wells-next-the-Sea
C29	East Coast of England Harwich to Whitby

Admiralty

1190	Flamborough Head to Blakeney Point
106	Cromer to Smiths Knoll
108	Approaches to the Wash
1200	The Wash Ports
1188	River Humber. Spurn Head to Immingham
3497	River Humber. Immingham to Humber Bridge & Rivers Ouse and Trent

Associated British Ports

River Humber
Spurn to Barton Haven

Barton Haven to Burton Stather

River Ouse
Apex Light to Skelton Bridge

From www.bcookeandson.co.uk
www.kildalemarine.co.uk

The Boating Association

www.theboatingassociation.co.uk

The River Ouse (Tidal) Naburn Lock to Trent Falls

Abbreviations and symbols

Abbreviations

Bn	Beacon	MMSI	Maritime Mobile Service Identity
By	Buoy	MSI	Maritime Safety Information incl. inshore waters forecast, gale warnings and navigational warnings
CC	Cruising Club	Mo	Morse
CG	Coastguard	N	North, Northwards, Northerly
Ch	Channel	NCB	North Cardinal Buoy
Conspic	Conspicuous	NCM	North Cardinal Mark (eg beacon)
DSC	Digital Selective Calling	NE	Northeast or Northeastwards
E	East, Eastwards, Easterly	NW	Northwest, Northwestwards
ECB	East Cardinal Buoy	Oc	Occulting light
ECM	East Cardinal Mark (eg beacon)	PHB	Port Hand Buoy
F	Fixed light	PHM	Port Hand Mark (eg beacon)
Fl	Flashing light	Pt	Point
ft	Foot, feet	PWC	Personal Water Craft (jet ski)
G	Green	Q	Quick flashing light
H	Hour, eg H+15 is 15 minutes past the hour	R	Red
hr	Hour, hours	S	South, Southwards, Southerly
HW	High Water	s	second(s)
HWN	High Water Neaps	SC	Sailing Club
HWS	High Water Springs	SCB	South Cardinal Buoy
IDM	Isolated Danger Mark	SCM	South Cardinal Mark (eg beacon)
IQ	Interrupted Quick flashing light	SHB	Starboard Hand Buoy
Iso	Isophase light	SHM	Starboard Hand Mark (eg beacon)
kn	Knot, knots	SW	Southwest, Southwestwards
L.Fl	Long flash	SWB	Safe Water Buoy
LNG	Liquefied Natural Gas	SWM	Safe Water Mark
LOA	Length Overall	TSS	Traffic Separation Scheme
LPG	Liquefied Petroleum Gas	UKHO	United Kingdom Hydrographic Office (the Admiralty)
LW	Low Water	UTC	Universal Time Corrected (same as GMT – Greenwich MeanTime)
LWN	Low Water Neaps	vert	vertical
LWS	Low Water Springs	VQ	Very Quick flashing light
M	Mile (nautical mile)	VTS	Vessel Traffic Service
m	metre	W	West, Westwards, Westerly; White
MHWS	Mean High Water springs	WCB	West Cardinal Buoy
min	Minute	WCM	West Cardinal Mark (eg beacon)
mins	Minutes	Y	Yellow
MLWS	Mean Low Water Springs	YC	Yacht Club

Small craft symbols

The following symbols are used on larger scale charts and plans:

- Visitors' moorings
- Visitors' berths
- Yacht marina
- Public landing
- Slipway for small craft
- Water tap
- Fuel
- Pump-out facilities
- Customs
- Public house, inn, bar
- Restaurant
- Yacht or sailing club
- Toilets
- Public car park
- Hard standing for boats
- Launderette
- Caravan site
- Camping site
- Nature reserve
- Harbourmaster
- Travel hoist
- Public telephone
- Post office
- Building
- Airport
- Flagpole/flagstaff
- Castle/Fort
- Hospital
- Notice Board
- Wooded
- Beacon (with various topmarks)
- Mooring buoy
- Crane
- Chimney
- Radio/TV Mast
- Water tower
- Tower
- Monument
- Wind turbine
- Tilting bridge

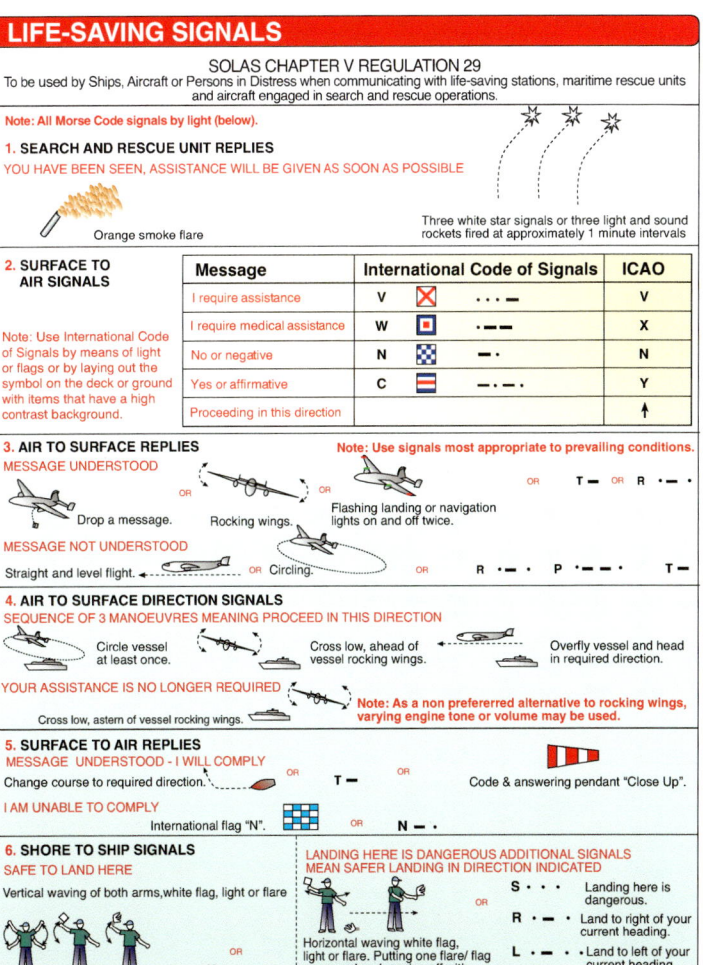

Norfolk, The Wash and Humber

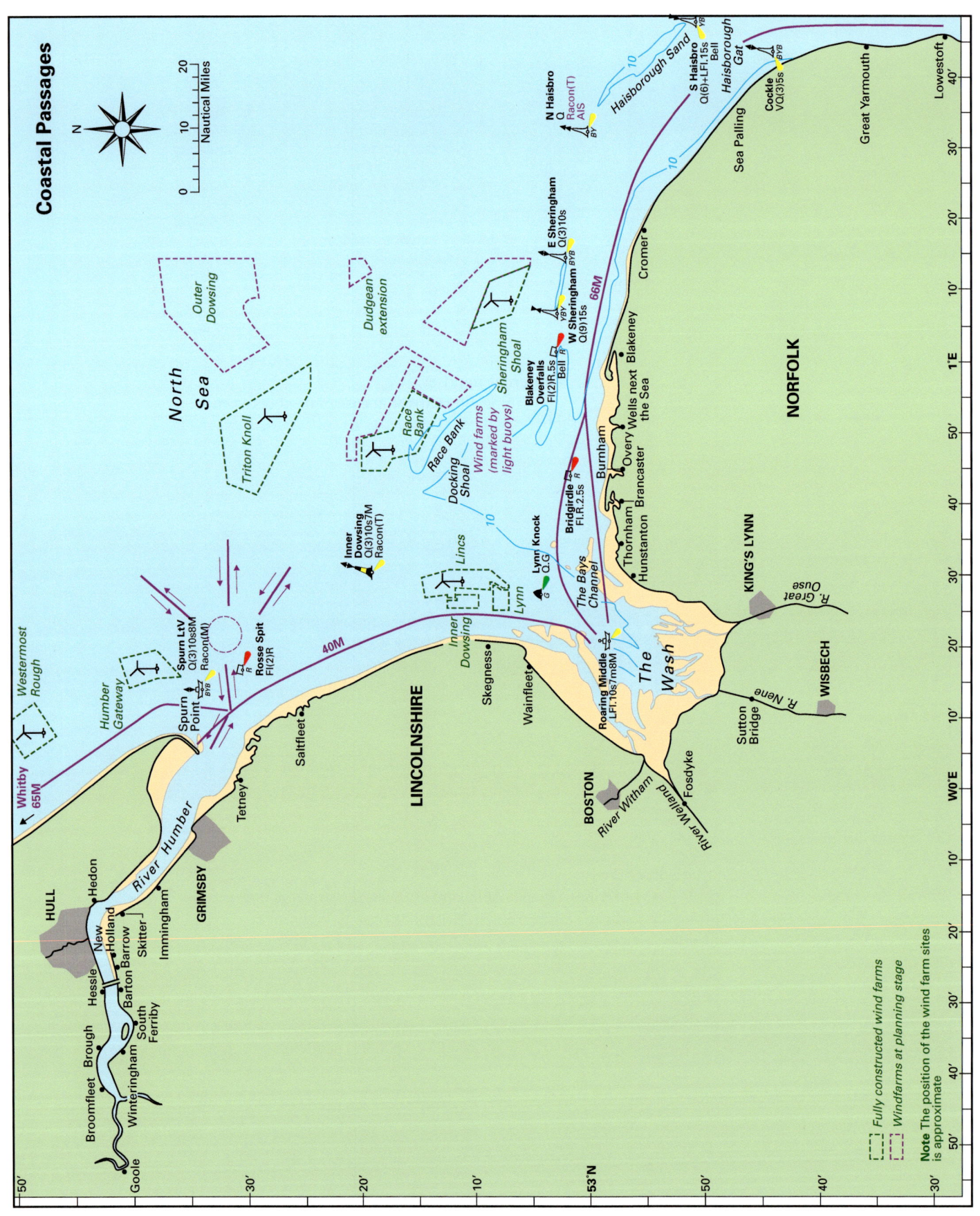

COASTAL PASSAGES

Sailing the waters of North Norfolk, The Wash and Humber, even for those who are new to them, should not present difficulty as long as their particular features are taken into account at an early stage. These being, for the most part, shoal waters and tides, although the region is not unique in that.

Of greatest importance is the fact that many rivers and harbours are tidally constrained, and it is essential to establish an optimum time for arrival. Clearly, after a long and arduous passage there is a desire to be alongside as early as possible and as soon as the tide permits. However, if entering a harbour for the first time, seek out local knowledge in advance – relevant links are given for each haven in the pages that follow. Even when there is sufficient depth for entry, there could still be value in an arrival when the tide is slack as in some locations, especially over springs, tidal rates in narrow channels can catch out the unwary.

It is undeniable that the stretch of the UK east coast between Lowestoft and Whitby is relatively devoid of marinas in the conventional sense. But it is not lacking in ports and anchorages or places of refuge, many of which accommodate sizeable commercial ships. Though, to take advantage of these requires a willingness to deviate from the rhumb line and in some cases, longer passages than in other regions. When tides are taken into account, these are not day sails.

For example, leaving Lowestoft and turning north means a passage of two tides to Wells-next-the-Sea, always assuming there is no north in the weather preventing entry across the bar. While a coasting passage 2-3M off on a summer day in a Force 4 from the north can be no more than a spirited sail, entering any of the Norfolk harbours, across sand banks and bars, some inter-tidal, is to encounter breaking waves and surf best left to those with boards designed for the purpose.

To then continue into The Wash for, say, the River Nene is the same distance as continuing up the coast to Grimsby, so marina hopping it is not.

North of Spurn Point too means a further 30M to Bridlington and, even then, the harbour is, for the most part, drying. Scarborough is another 15M and remaining afloat, while possible, needs negotiating. Not until Whitby, another 13M distant, is the standard marina offer available. Just for context, Spurn Point to Whitby is another two-tide passage. So, to summarise, cruising between Lowestoft and Whitby requires a different mindset.

Having alternatives in case of need between origin and destination is more than just sensible and several anchorages allow some options. Most of these have been in use for centuries, so why not put them to use? They are, after all, free!

Even if one's preference is for passage making, a pause for respite when the weather is less favourable can often be prudent. Pressing on takes its toll on boat and occupants.

In most places, as long as someone knows your plan, there can be help at hand when you arrive. In any case, in most locations it is essential to check berth availability in advance. While all the moorings are first class, and a perfect link with the region's many attractions, arriving to find there is nowhere to moor can be more than an embarrassment, as returning to sea might not be an option once the tide is away.

To Wells-next-the-Sea

For most leisure cruisers, the strategic port on the North Norfolk coast is Wells-next-the-Sea.

From the south

Perhaps Lowestoft as a last port, is a coasting passage of 56M to Wells. Midway is Sea Palling, a traditional anchorage where a reef close inshore is marked with PH beacons. Factors to take account of would be any preference to carry tide through Yarmouth Road rather than push it, but arrival at the Wells fairway buoy needs to be coincident with sufficient height of tide to cross the bar. Alternative waiting anchorages are immediately north of the Wells fairway WCM or in Holkham Bay close and to the west.

'Rolling Roads'

This section of the book has 'rolling road' diagrams to assist pilotage.

Read each rolling road from the bottom upwards.

The long blue arrow through the middle of the diagram shows which buoys are to be left to port and which to starboard.

The angled short blue arrows tell the helmsman the general direction to take towards or from a particular buoy, until the navigator works out the exact new course.

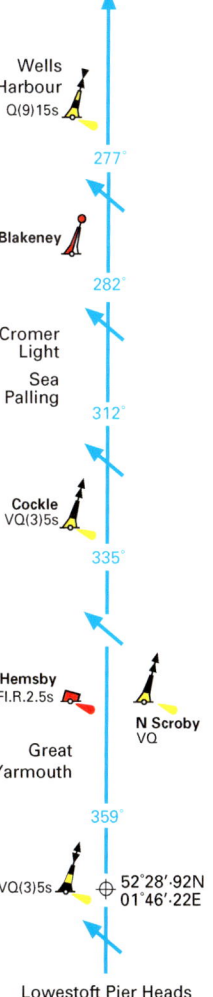

Lowestoft towards North Norfolk havens and The Wash ports

Norfolk, The Wash and Humber

Towards North Norfolk and The Wash from the North Sea south of 53° N

From the North Sea

Towards the North Norfolk coast, a course will depend on whether coming from north or south of 53°N.

If the former then W of North Haisborough NCM Q. Racon (T).

If south then via Smiths Knoll SCM Q(6)+LFl.15s Racon (T) and then Haisborough Gat.

From The Wash

Eastwards there is a recently surveyed passage off Gore Point and through The Bays which cuts a corner via 53°0'·000N 000°30'·660E. The area to avoid would be Bridgirdle shoal, some of which dries, but a passage via the Bridgirdle PHM Fl.R 2.5s achieves this.

From the north

Will be along the Lincolnshire coast then between Race Bank and Docking Shoal and at the South Race SCM Q(6)+LFl.15s either crossing Blakeney Overfalls or rounding the eponymous PHM Fl(2)R 5s. Direction of tide may have a bearing and the flood runs eastward, although rates are not great here. From Grimsby it is 52M to Wells.

Towards The Wash

From the south

A likely approach for many will be a coastal passage from Lowestoft, from where the entry to The Wash will be approximately 66M. On into Wisbech, as one example, is 97M.

Sailing north out of Lowestoft, the rate of tide through Yarmouth Roads is not to be underestimated. Having some north going stream is an important consideration until your course has some westing in it. Thereafter, deep enough water is to be found 2M or so offshore and, if the wind is off the land, a smooth passage results. An eye on the echo sounder remains a requirement nonetheless, as well as a good lookout for crab and lobster pots, especially off Cromer and Sheringham. Some of these can carry little by way of top marks, and if the passage is at night, particular vigilance is recommended. A rope around a propellor can spoil an enjoyable sail in an instant.

Early in the passage, which might suit if tide is adverse, it is an option to anchor off Sea Palling, where the Norfolk coast begins to fall away westward. The location is easily identified with a reef marked by PH beacons.

The church tower is conspicuous. Assuming Wells was your interim goal, and if early on a tide, further passage anchorages are shown on the charts in both Wells Road and Holkham Bay. Not advisable if the wind is, or has been, in the north but under these circumstances Wells may not be tenable in any case.

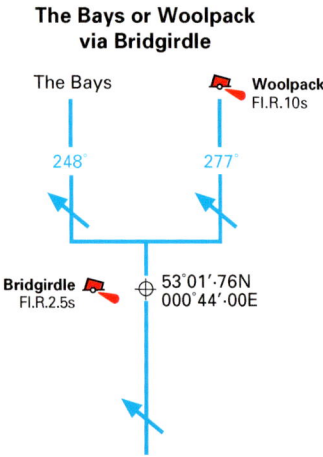

From Wells to The Bays or Woolpack via Bridgirdle

From the WCM marking the start of the Wells approach channel, it is then 12M to the Woolpack PHM on the southeast corner of The Wash proper. Shaping a course via Bridgirdle PHM and leaving it to port is advised as the Bridgirdle shoal remains a consideration. This shallower area has been around for a long time with little change, which says much for its consistency. In places it dries.

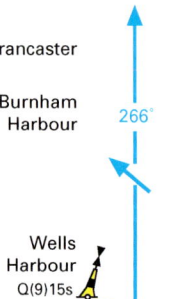

From Wells via The Bays Inshore Passage

An inshore passage through The Bays is possible, leaving Gore Middle and Middle Bank to starboard which brings into play The Bays anchorage, especially if shelter is required. The sandbanks are excellent breakwaters and have been used as such for centuries. However, while this inshore route is attractive, leaving Bridgirdle PHM to port should remain part of the plan unless draught is a lesser consideration, but even then, not on a falling tide.

Thereafter and upon entering The Wash, the Roaring Middle SWM LFl 10s in 52°58'·63N 000°21'·03E is the usual waypoint from where a course can be laid for whichever of the ports is the final objective.

From the north

There's every chance that your last port of call will have been either Grimsby or Hull. Grimsby to Wisbech is 68M. In any case, Spurn Head will be your tide-influenced point of departure for passages towards The Wash from the north.

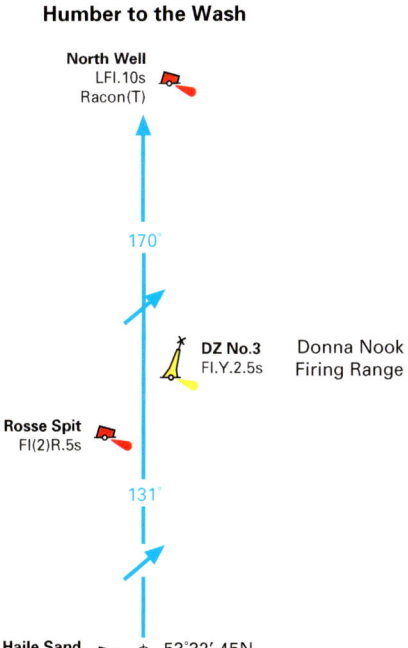

Time your passage to carry the flood tide into The Wash to arrive at your destination at local high water. Given it is approximately 40M from Spurn to the Roaring Middle LF, this can mean some adverse tide or a preparedness to kill time either at anchor or hove to.

A course keeping more than 3M offshore is fairly straightforward but should be shaped outside the Donna Nook bombing range yellow DZ buoys, for obvious reasons. When active, a listening watch is kept by the range control on VHF 16. Note too the extent of Haile Sand Flat which dries closer inshore.

Safe havens en-route are non-existent for all practical purposes. While there are tidal moorings in Saltfleet Haven, without good local knowledge and a boat which can take the ground, this is not an option.

Nearing The Wash, keep landward of the Lynn and Inner Dowsing wind farms which make fine visual targets, especially towards the end of a passage. The southwest corner of Lynn windfarms marks the point of decision over approach, which will be conditioned by objective and weather.

From offshore

For the visitor from further afield, perhaps from the European mainland or even the Baltic, approaching The Wash after a North Sea crossing presents a different prospect, not least because of extensive offshore sands, knolls, banks and ridges, the channels through which run principally NW/SE.

Numerous oil and gas platforms are further obstacles. These structures do, nonetheless, offer relief from an otherwise featureless seascape and assist in position fixing. In addition, conventional aids to navigation abound, many of which are Racon, or increasingly, AIS beacons. In general, charted depths are not great and overfalls can occur.

Bridgirdle PHM in a calm

Final approach to the Wash. St. Edmund's Point, Hunstanton

From north of 53°N a suitable passage is less obstructed. South of this line of latitude less so, but leaving Smiths Knoll SCM Q(6)LFl.15s (52°43'·53N 002°17'·90E) to starboard, then shaping a course through Haisborough Gat closes the coast towards Cromer, when the passage becomes a more straightforward, coasting one.

Within The Wash

The deep-water route into The Wash after leaving the Lynn and Inner Dowsing wind farms is via Lynn Knock SHM and North Well SWM, a prominent navigation aid and Racon. This is the logical passage if either King's Lynn (River Great Ouse) or Wisbech (River Nene) are the objectives, although it serves all ports via the respective, well buoyed approach channels.

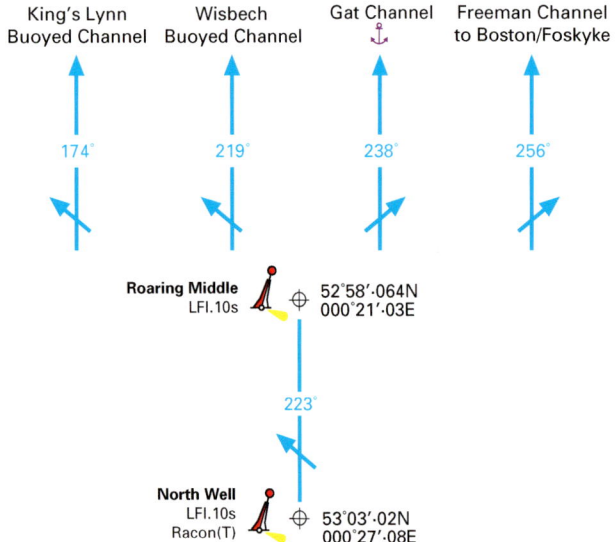

From North Well towards The Wash Ports and buoyed approach channels

A quick study of the chart (UKHO 1200, Imray Y9) will serve to reassure over depths in The Wash, which are considerable when clear of the inter-tidal areas. For those mariners with lingering doubts over entering The Wash embayment, note that it is not unusual to find extremely large, ocean-going ships using it for temporary shelter.

Even if the weather is, or has been, brisk from the north or northeast, an approach to Sutton Bridge can be made after half tide rising, and good shelter can be found in almost any conditions. Being driven onto a lee shore should not be a source of worry.

If Boston or Fosdyke is the aim, then it is perfectly valid to continue into Boston Deep leaving Outer Dogs Head to port. Be advised, however, that this route has long since been un-buoyed. Nevertheless, recent surveys have shown it to be entirely viable given use of the latest chart. Around local LW but on a rising tide is a good time in that uncovered sands are a simpler prospect, although weather, particularly wind direction, is an important consideration.

Worthy of mention here is Wainfleet Haven, home to the Gibraltar Point Sailing Club. See page 54.

This inshore route leads naturally to Lower Road and from the Freeman Channel there is good buoyage, this being the approach channel for the port of Boston (River Witham) as well as Fosdyke (River Welland). Tabs Head is the junction of these two rivers. If early, an anchorage to await the tide is possible to landward of the PHM Foxtrot, but be mindful to keep well to landward and thus clear of Boston commercial shipping.

Inward passage from Tabs Head will be governed by destination. If Boston, then be advised that entering the Witham without having made berthing arrangements in advance is not recommended. Below the Grand Sluice sea lock there are no all-afloat moorings, and entering the commercial dock basins is not an option. Above the sluice, non-tidal mooring options exist but the air draught is limited.

To the River Humber

From the south

The low-lying Lincolnshire coast to the south of the Humber mouth is generally featureless and offers little by way of radar target. Upon closing the Humber, areas to avoid include a number of overfalls and the Donna Nook Firing Range extending up to 6M to seaward. When active, this military air weapons range keeps a listening watch on VHF 16. It is clearly marked by yellow DZ buoys. Navigate outside this zone when active. Full details of range activity can be found at: www.gov.uk/government/publications/military-low-flying-air-weapons-ranges-activity/air-weapons-ranges-normal-opening-times

Also keep to seaward of the DZ No.3 buoy Fl.Y.2.5s which also serves to clear Rosse Spit. Depths vary here and over Haile Sand Flat.

Rosse Spit PHM Fl(2)R.5s marks the outward lane of the Rosse Reach TSS. Here entry to the Humber begins in earnest. At this point, the recommended small craft track

keeps south of the commercial ship buoyed channels and leads towards Grimsby.

For the northern bank, Hull Marina for example, crossing the separation zones will be necessary. Crossing on a course of approximately 032°, between Charlie and Bravo Light Floats to the No.3 Chequer SCM.

From here, a course north of west, either within or skirting the east bound edge of the separation zone clears Spurn Point after 3M and leads to either Bull or Hawke buoyed channels.

From the north

The Humber Gateway Wind Farm to the east of Spurn Head will likely be the first visual indication of the mouth of the Humber and shaping a course to the south and west of this feature will bring you to the New Sand Hole separation zone, SW inbound lane.

A southerly course towards the Spurn Light Float Q(3)10s8M Racon(M) should avoid the Outer Binks where rough, broken seas can occur, especially with wind against tide. The Inner Binks, to the east and north of Spurn Head and extending 2.5M to seaward, has areas which can dry at low water. This area too experiences rough, broken seas and should be avoided.

From the Spurn LF, a course of 258° takes you along the northern edge of the separation zone for 2M to the No.3 Chequer SCM. If the intention is to anchor behind Spurn Head or proceed upstream to Hull Marina or any other north bank destination, skirting the separation zone on a course of 293° clears Spurn Head after 3M, when either the Bull or Hawke channels can be taken according to preference. In any case, informing Humber VTS (Ch. 14 here) of intentions will ensure awareness of any relevant shipping movements, especially to and from the Bull Anchorage.

If the intended destination is, for example, Grimsby on the south bank, then from the No.3 Chequer SCM, the recommendation is to turn to the south, entering the cautionary zone to cross the separation scheme and pass between the Charlie and Bravo RW Fairway Light Floats. It is highly recommended that before entering the cautionary zone, contact is made with Humber VTS on VHF 14. No.2B PHM Fl.R.4s is the start of the recommended track for small craft and wind farm service vessels.

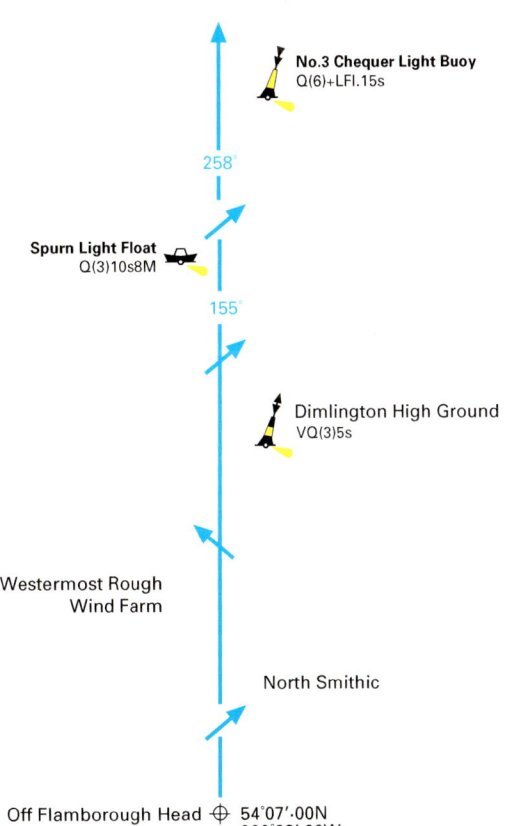

Low water, summer equinox and still coasting along The Freeman Channel into Boston Deep

Norfolk, The Wash and Humber

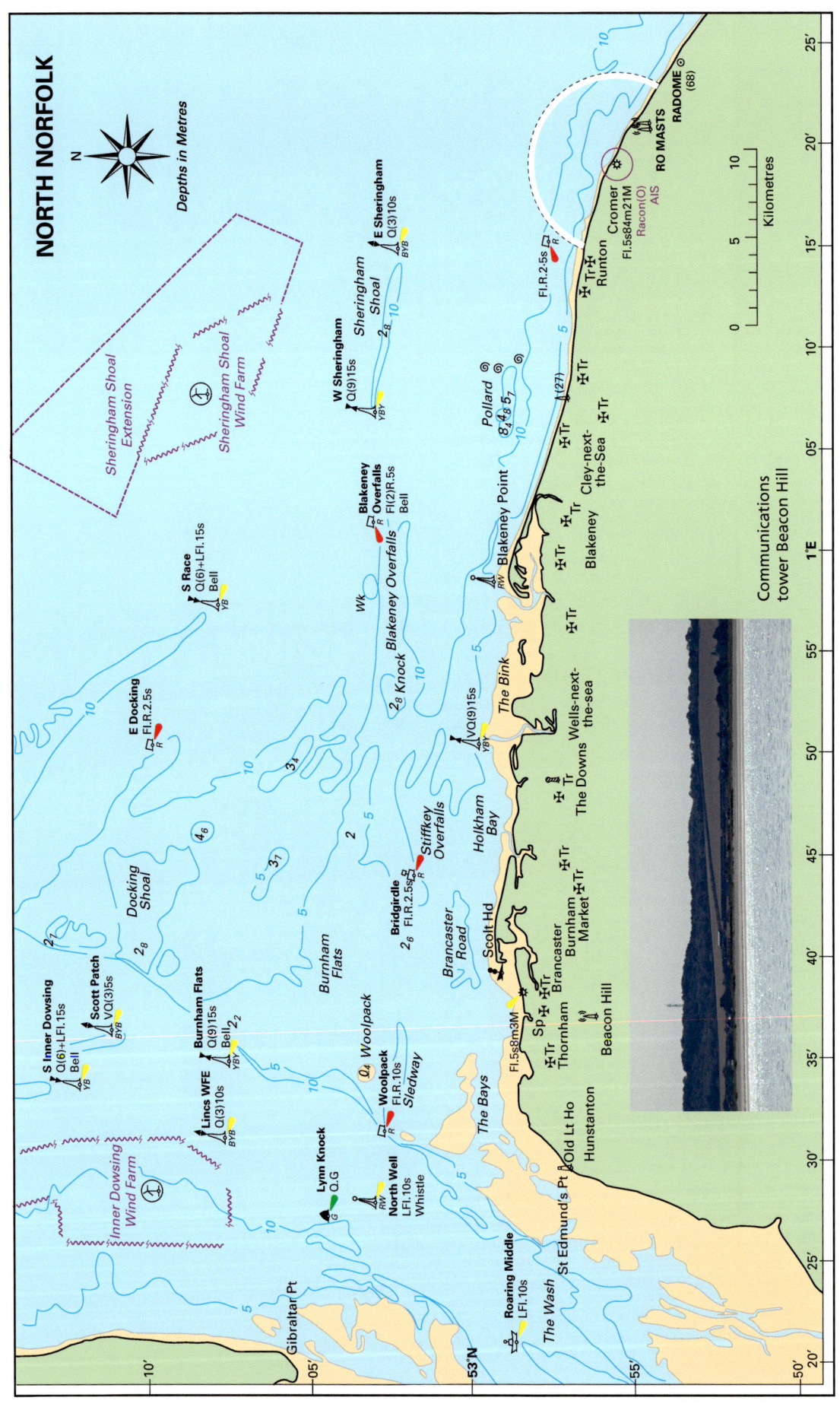

14

NORTH NORFOLK

The areas covered by this pilot each have their characteristics from both land and sea and North Norfolk is no exception. It has a reputation for being flat, yet those who subscribe to this view have clearly never cycled around it. And while coastal features do not include towering cliffs, an inshore passage here will not disappoint for want of scenic attraction. With a rich maritime heritage, North Norfolk still turns its face to the sea via its drying harbours and creeks. Inshore commercial fishing and aquaculture influence character as does the area's international importance for wildlife and habitats. Enjoyment ashore is enhanced through two national walking trails. Part of the English Coast Path runs here, as do Peddars Way and the Norfolk Coast Path, through an Area of Outstanding Natural Beauty. Recreational activity abounds and includes bird watching, angling, open-water swimming, board and paddle sports and diving and snorkelling. A trawl through www.wnnmp.co.uk reveals more.

For the visitor by boat, between Cromer to the east and Gore Point to the west is a mixture of low cliff leading to a shingle strip guarding sandy inlets, then offlying dunes providing natural wave barriers on this north facing coast. Vast, open beaches give way to salt marshes as the direction changes to lead into the Wash. The general picture is of movement, siltation and erosion and, while welcoming, the harbours which remain are suitable only for craft which can take the ground. Even then, not if weather has been from the north. Under these conditions, entry across harbour bars can be dangerous. The gem on this stretch is Wells-next-the-Sea where visitor facilities are excellent, although again, caution is the watchword for entry in all but benign sea states.

Tides by and large follow the coast and rates are not great, but distances demand planning. If underpowered for any reason, anchoring should be a consideration. Given that prevailing winds are offshore, this is not without its attraction. Traditional anchorages are indicated on both Admiralty and Imray charts and holding is good. Landmarks are to be found and buoyage is sufficient to the task. Cromer light and its pier make for excellent reference. Church towers and spires are conspicuous, as is Scolt Head Island and, west of here, communications masts on The Downs and Beacon Hill. The windmill inland of Holme next the Sea is at 55m. West of Cromer there are fewer offlying dangers, save for occasional overfalls and a multitude of lobster and crab pots liable to trap the unwary.

Surf's up at Cromer in a Northerly Force 4

Norfolk, The Wash and Humber

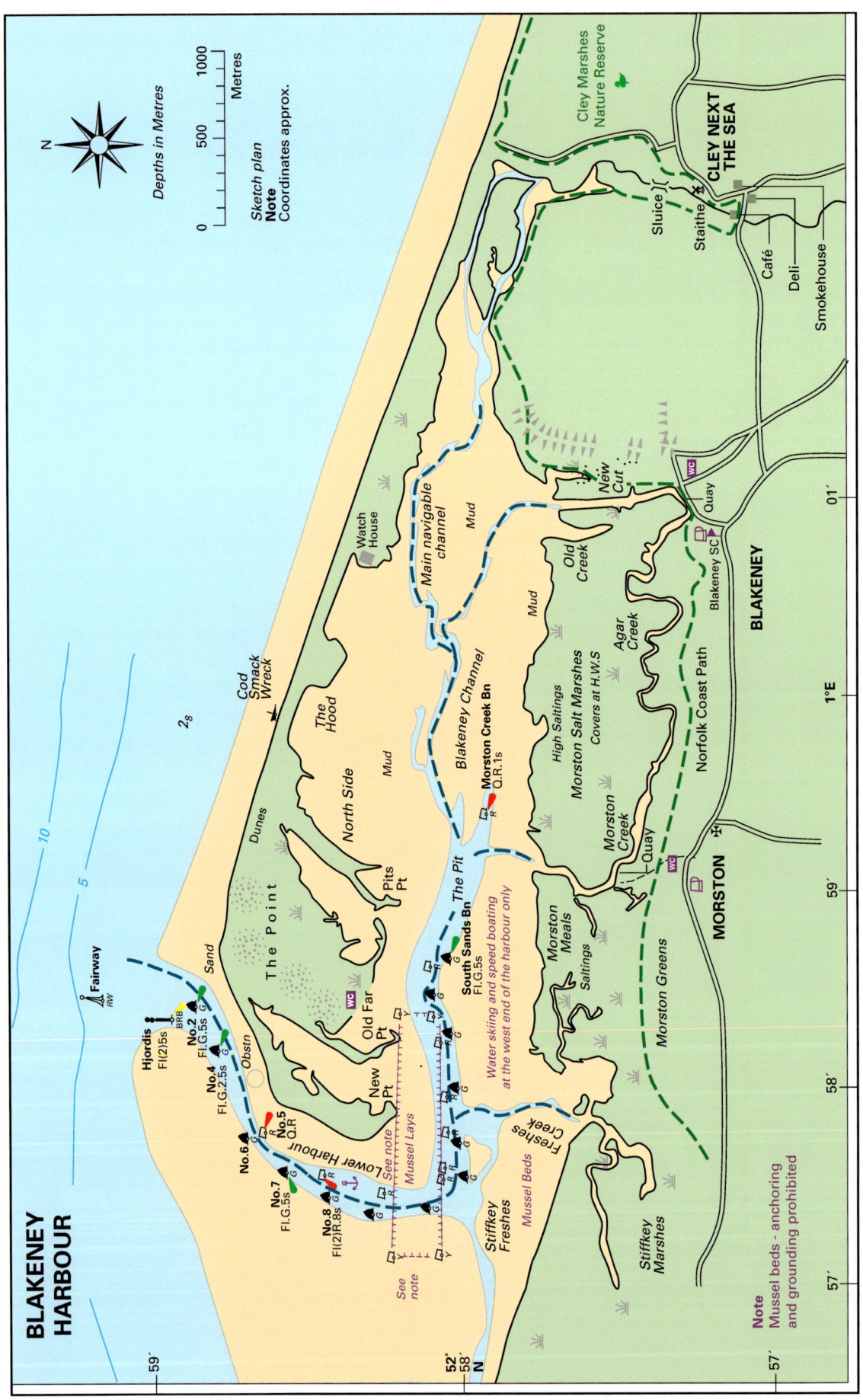

TIDAL HAVENS OF NORTH NORFOLK

Blakeney Harbour

⊕ 52°59'·17N 000°58'·48E
Blakeney Harbour safe water mark

'Blakeney is a small Town which lye into a small creek ten miles from Foulness. Blakeney is a great church and a high, square steeple; bring the church south east and run in so into five or six Fathom water till you see the buoys; there is but half a fathom of water at low water.'

So reads *Great Britain's Coasting Pilot* of 1693, so any mariner visiting Blakeney is buying into the centuries of maritime history which make this coast so fascinating.

But as with all the North Norfolk havens, save for Wells-next-the-Sea, unless one is cruising in a small, shoal draught yacht, one with a lifting keel or a multi-hull, Blakeney is, sadly, best avoided from seaward.

If planning a visit from sea however, consulting the Blakeney Harbour Association (BHA) early is essential. The harbour is managed by local volunteers and while welcoming, North Norfolk is no longer a sleepy string of bucolic hamlets. The seasonal population is considerable and harbour activity no exception. In addition, all moorings are drying.

The harbour entrance from the open sea must be treated with caution. If there is, or has been, south in the wind all should be well, but winds from other directions, especially north and east, create considerable swell over the bar when an entry would be unwise.

Having said all that, the marine visitor spending time in North Norfolk will be missing much if Blakeney is not on an itinerary, one way or another.

Blakeney comes into its own during the summer season as a magnet for the day sailor, whether with dinghy, kayak or even a trailable cabin boat. The creeks and swatchways and the abundant wildlife make this area a haven for any discerning boater prepared to get their feet wet.

The whole area is part of The Wash and North Norfolk European Marine Partnership, a European Marine Site protected in legislation for its nature and very essence. The small craft mariner here will therefore be sharing the habitat with a wide range of other interests; flora, fauna and human. A look at www.wnnmp.co.uk is recommended.

Useful information – Blakeney

Fairway buoy Unlit Spherical RW 52° 59'·17N 000°58'·48E
Isolated Danger BRB Hjordis Fl.2 5s. 52° 59'·02N 000°58'·14E

Moorings All moorings dry. Anchoring is an option but seek local advice. Channel is marked but winding. Minimal shoreside facility.

Contacts
Harbour Authority Blakeney Harbour Association (BHA)
☎ +44 7929 181138 ☎ +44 1263 741172 Call in advance.
www.blakeneyharbourassociation.co.uk for chartlet and pilotage advice. Also see website for prevailing weather and sea state conditions.
Alternative contact numbers for advice in advance of entry
☎ +44 7786 092405 / ☎ +44 7795 463943

VHF Port Working Channel No dedicated channel.

Tidal predictions based on Wells.

Hazards Positions of buoys are liable to change. Entry may not be viable in or after N / NE winds. Optimum time for entry depends on draught, tidal height and intentions.

Charts Admiralty 108, 1503 Imray Y9, C28

Approaches

See plan page 14

For most, the approach to Blakeney will be a coasting one. That is not to say it cannot be approached from seaward. Just a matter of probability. From offshore an approach is less easy given off-lying dangers and the lack of buoyage other than the lateral marks close in. But the Sheringham Shoal wind farm does represent a useful visual reference. Thereafter the West Sheringham WCB Q(9)15s and a course of 232° for approximately 6M brings up the Blakeney Harbour SWM fairway buoy which is unlit.

Closer in is the Hjordis IDM FL(2)5s, inward of which the serpentine channel and the harbour area are marked with some 50 or so buoys, most of which are lit. Ashore there is a lack of features save for St. Nicholas' church tower which bears 163° from Hjordis.

Entry

The local advice is for an entry over HW +/- 1hr on springs only. At neaps there is little or no access. Furthermore, check the swell conditions before committing and on no account attempt to enter or leave outside HW

Norfolk, The Wash and Humber

All moorings dry at Blakeney
Gary Garford

+/- 2hrs. Tidal range is small. It is worth seeking local advice for a chosen day, if available.

Numerous lateral marks lie inward of the Hjordis IDM and the channel begins by running approximately southwest then at the No.6 SHM turns to the south and at the 12A PHM, to the east. The positions of buoys can vary. A full list of buoys and their positions can be obtained from the Blakeney Harbour Association website. See 'Useful information'.

The channel divides where creeks from first Stiffkey then Morston join, and ultimately the River Glaven running from Cley next the Sea. The Glaven has some aids to navigation. Channels to Stiffkey and Morston are less well marked.

The main channel terminates at Blakeney Quay, the landward extremity of the town.

Moorings

All laid moorings dry. Most, if not all, are occupied by local boats but some can be available to visitors upon asking. Clearly, if a visiting boat is content to take the ground and the intention is to spend time ashore, the shorter the walk the better and once dried out, there is more time available to be enjoyed ashore. To book a mooring, call the BHA. A modest charge is payable, £10.00 per night at the time of writing.

Any notion of mooring alongside Morston or Blakeney quays is discouraged. Blakeney Quay is very congested and the boats there can be three abreast. The quay is not in the control of the BHA. Additionally, there are passenger boat operators who run harbour tours and some of the quay is allocated to them. Harbour trips ply to and from Morston too and no spare section of quay is available there. Visitors should gain shore access over these quays by tender only.

Anchoring

Anchoring is permitted, free of charge, although a donation to the BHA is appreciated. Taking advice over to where to drop the hook is sensible, at least to avoid some steep-to locations.

Remaining afloat at anchor within Blakeney Harbour can be possible, subject to draught and height of tide. The first possibility is immediately inward of Blakeney Bar and the lateral marks SHM No.2, SHM No.4 and PHM No.5. To its seaward end, this area, known as Lower Harbour, appears as open sea at HW but come half tide, sand banks to the east and west and the bar to the north form natural breakwaters.

Blakeney Pit, to the west end of Lower Harbour, is more sheltered and has the deepest water but parts do still dry at LW and local knowledge should be sought before setting off in the tender or turning in for the night. There is generally less effect from swell when anchored in Blakeney Pit.

Facilities

As the popularity of North Norfolk has grown over recent decades, the visitor is well catered for. Most gastronomic tastes can be satisfied and the pub lunch, wherever one seeks it, can be as simple or sophisticated as required. Everything from basic provisions to artisanal, niche produce is on hand.

In Blakeney there are public toilets opposite the quay car park and there is a unisex facility in the village hall carpark nearer to the main coast road. Morston has a public toilet and there are some portable units in the National Trust car park. No public facility in Stiffkey or Cley.

Petrol and diesel are available from the garage in Blakeney. Water cans can be filled nearby and general waste disposed of. There are marine trades in both Blakeney and Morston and some chandlery. In case of need, boats can be recovered over conventional slipways.

Visitor information

For the visitor who enjoys pottering around swatchway and salting, exploring in the tender with the aid of an outboard is a delight here. As with most North Norfolk villages, Stiffkey and Morston offer much. Cley next the Sea, thanks to the Cley Harbour Project, now has its quay reinstated and following the Glaven as it twists inward will be well rewarded. The BHA recommends walking the channels at LW by way of personal surveys, before a visit by water, which is pleasant recreation in any case.

In terms of things to do, visitors to the area are, in the main, seeking outdoor pursuits which include birdwatching and walking. The North Norfolk Coastal Path is here and the National Trust manages nature reserves in the vicinity. There are other local attractions; Holkham Hall for example and Sheringham and Cromer, the region's seaside towns. These are beyond walking distance but can be accessed on the bus.

Blakeney
Gary Garford

Wells-next-the-Sea

Here we have, unquestionably, a gem. Wells has adapted successfully to change more than many and it remains a vibrant harbour, still with commercial interests, though the dominant scene is one of small boats.

Essentially another drying harbour with sand that doesn't sit still but, thanks to the diligence of the harbour authority, visiting Wells is straightforward. And the bonus is remaining afloat at the excellent visitor pontoon in the heart of the waterfront. The town of Wells has never turned its back on the sea and waterborne activity is at the centre of everything.

A seaport since the 1300s, Wells had great prominence for grain shipments to London

---

Useful information – Wells-next-the-Sea

Fairway buoy WCM 52°59'·70N 000° 50'·19E

Moorings All tide visitor pontoon. Otherwise, harbour dries. Full shoreside facilities.

Contacts ☏ +44 1328 711646 Call in advance with ETA. *Harbour Authority* Port of Wells. www.wellsharbour.co.uk See website for chartlet and pilotage advice. Printed harbour guide on request.

VHF Port Working Channel 12. Call 'Wells Harbour' from sea on approach.

Tidal predictions based on Wells.

Hazards Entry possibly not viable in or after N / NE winds. Entry >HW +/- 3hr subject to draught and tidal height. Consult Harbour Office for tide reading and sea state across the bar.

Charts Admiralty 108, 1503. Imray Y9, C28

Wells inward guided by the harbour launch *Mark Ashley-Miller*

and the northeast from where coal was imported. It was also once a centre of malt production, with a significant trade to the Netherlands in particular. Commercial fishing has long featured too, and a small fleet of inshore boats still works from here. Always something going on.

Tourism is now highly important to the local economy and the development of the facility for visiting leisure vessels establishes Wells as somewhere not to be missed during a summer cruise.

The strategic value of Wells is that it does not require a great diversion from an east coast transit, and for visitors from northern Europe it's amongst the nearest options after a North Sea crossing.

Approaches

The optimum course to steer for Wells will be a mostly straightforward decision, whether the passage is a coasting one or from offshore. Timing will depend on point of origin and whether to push foul tide or anchor, a matter of preference after an assessment of wind and sea state. A passage to Wells is not a day sail save for those with lots of horse power. (See page 9.)

Entry

Prior notice of entry is greatly preferred by the harbour authority. The visitor pontoon is not large, so an enquiry as to berth availability is a sensible and seamanlike precaution.

While the coast is low lying it is not devoid of visual references and immediately to the west of the harbour entrance is a conspicuous pine plantation known as Holkham Meals.

Entry is across a sand bar which is subject to change. Optimum time for entry will vary according to draught and tidal height.

On springs, vessels drawing up to 3m can enter at HW, but on neaps only up to 1.75m draught. Tidal range is small and strong winds from any direction can cause variation from predictions (see page 2). Enquiry of the harbour office will give real time tide gauge readings.

Strong winds from the north or east can render entry unviable, as can residual sea state, even if winds from those directions have abated. Seek local advice.

For entry at night, or if unsure, the harbour launch may be available to escort vessels,

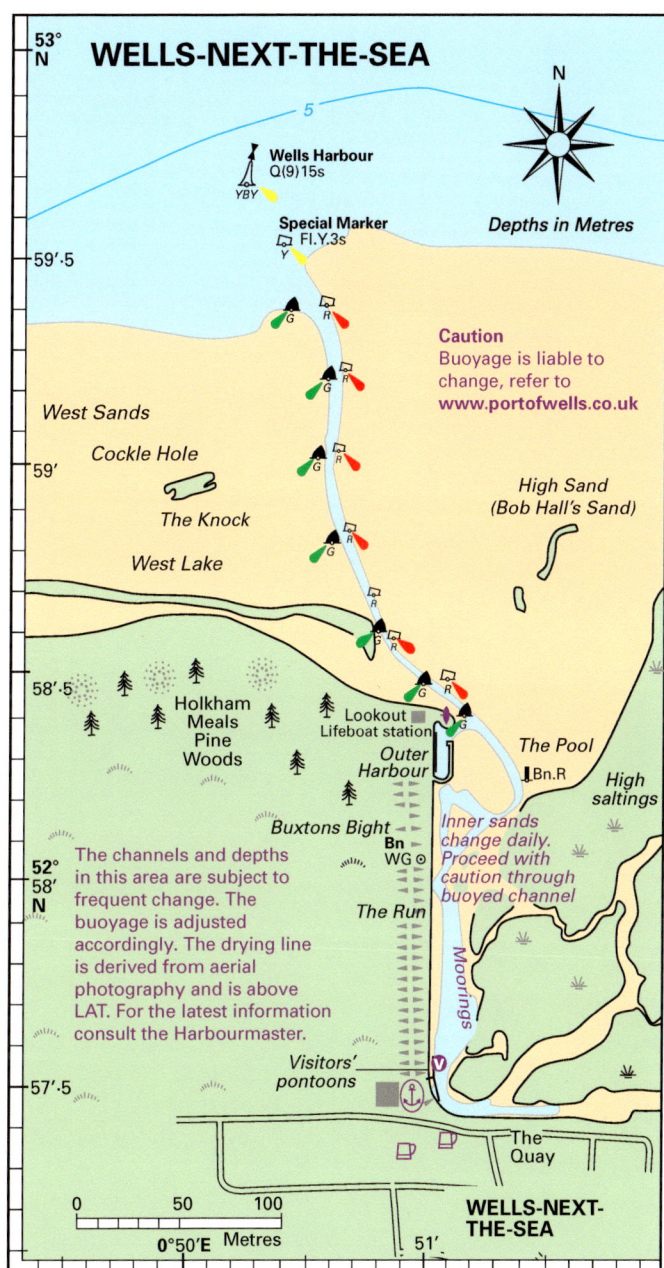

Sea Horse, Wells

Norfolk, The Wash and Humber

The excellent visitor pontoon in the heart of Wells waterfront, looking seaward
Mark Ashley-Miller

Drying moorings above Wells quay
Gary Garford

even up to the quayside. Note however that harbour staff availability is seasonally affected.

If conditions appear favourable, leave the fairway WCM on a course of 165/170° towards the yellow Special Mark (Fl.Y 3s), leaving it to port. Continue to the SHM No.1 (Fl.G 3s) and PHM No.2 (Fl.R3s) laid as a pair. Thereafter the channel errs towards the starboard shore line, through a succession of smaller lateral marks, before curving southwards again to the red roofed lifeboat station and the outer harbour, both on a starboard hand promontory.

Many of the channel marks are lit but their characteristics are similar; Fl.R or Fl.G 3s.

This outer harbour, constructed for wind farm maintenance and supply vessels servicing Sheringham Shoal wind farm, is continually dredged, as is the access channel. Keep clear of craft engaged in this activity.

During summer months the beaches are very busy and the usual range of holiday activities are encountered close at hand, including swimmers.

After the lifeboat station, the buoyed channel deviates towards the east shore and round a bight before returning west and then running mainly south along the beach line. Here there are moorings to port, and a beach to starboard, from which, again, swimmers can be encountered.

Ahead now is the town with the visitor pontoon to starboard next to the harbour office. If the tide still floods, run past and turn before coming alongside, port side to.

For a local pilotage guide with a difference, see www.portofwells/navigation/video

Moorings

In addition to the berths on the well-appointed visitor pontoon, alternative berths

can be available on the quay wall. Swinging fore and aft moorings are also available, but these may dry. Anchoring is also permitted for no charge, although not in a fairway. Consult the harbour office.

In 2022, mooring charges on quay and pontoon were £1 per foot (0.3m) LOA per night with a minimum of £24.00. It is highly unlikely that mooring in the outer harbour will be permitted, and in any event this is close to 1M from the town.

Facilities

The visitor pontoon is fully serviced with power and water. Showers and toilets, washing machine and dryer are on the barge adjacent to the pontoon.

The boating visitor to Wells is unlikely to want for anything. Given the accent on maritime life, the attendant trades are in the vicinity and boat building and boat machinery repair go on locally. Standard House Chandlery is on the quayside and diesel is available from the dedicated berth, on the tide.

Wells now boasts a 35T slipway hoist and vessels can be recovered, by arrangement, for repair or maintenance.

Visitor information

The town is compact so can be toured easily on foot and its history, ancient and not so ancient, is worthy of curiosity. Small commercial vessels were built here until the late 19th century and even the coming of the railways didn't completely end the coastal shipping trade. The quayside granary, now flats, was active until 1990. John Fryer, William Bligh's sailing master in HMS Bounty, was born in Wells and survived the epic, post mutiny boat journey, and probably much more. He is buried in St. Nicholas' churchyard.

Nearby is Holkham Hall, ancestral home to successive Earls of Leicester, and for those wishing to venture beyond town boundaries, offers considerable variety from house, grounds and seasonal events. Coastal walks await those wishing to exercise and the coastal bus service, to King's Lynn in one direction and Cromer the other, opens up much of North Norfolk if other havens are impracticable. www.visitnorthnorfolk.co.uk

Burnham Overy Harbour

Burnham Overy, one of the North Norfolk villages known collectively as 'The Burnhams', is perhaps most notable for its staithe. Its name, 'Overy' meaning 'Over the river,' relates specifically to the River Burn. And not far inland is Burnham Thorpe, the birthplace of Horatio Nelson who, according to local records, learnt to row and sail from Burnham Overy Staithe.

In centuries past, Burnham Overy itself was the port for the Burnham villages but with the silting of the river, commercial traffic switched to the Staithe downstream and with the subsequent coming of the railway, ceased altogether in the early 1900s.

Entering Burnham Overy with Scolt Head Island to starboard
Ash Faire-Ring

Useful information – Burnham Overy Staithe

Fairway buoy Entry is between Gun Hill and the east end of Scolt Head Island.

Buoyed channel Trinity House maintain 2 SHM and 3PHM to seaward (unlit) but the entrance moves. Once inside, groynes to each hand are marked which indicate the channel course.

Moorings Many laid moorings which can be used with permission. Anchoring an option. Harbour dries.

Contacts Harbour Warden (seasonal availability only) email jejmarine@gmail.com
In emergency, ☏ +44 7960 280139.
Harbour Authority Burnham Overy Harbour, a charitable trust.
www.burnhamoveryharbour.com

VHF Port Working Channel No dedicated channel.

Tidal predictions based on Wells.

Hazards Offshore winds can render entry unviable. Entry according to draught and height of tide close to local HW. Ebb runs strongly.

Charts Admiralty 108 Imray Y9

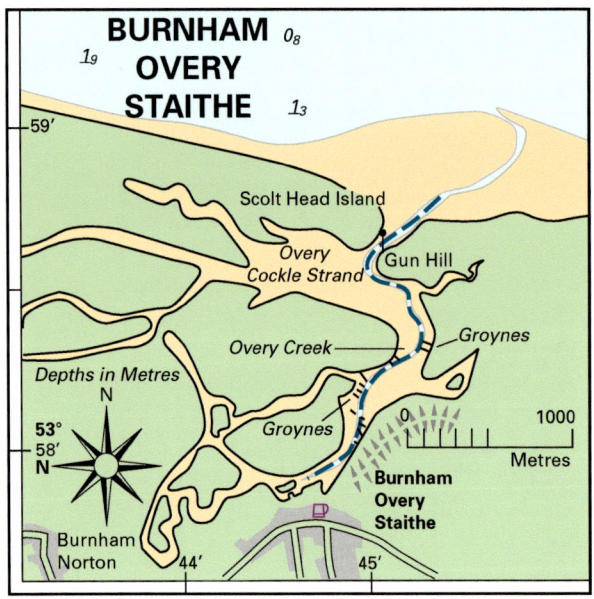

Today, this attractive drying harbour is a centre of much small craft activity, both leisure and fishing. While not a prospect for every cruising yacht, those prepared and able to take the ground can visit Burnham to great advantage. The day sailor, wishing to launch over a tide, would be hard pressed to find greater enjoyment than from pottering around the creeks and salt marshes around Burnham. Similarly, if you are RIB coasting North Norfolk, by all means nose into Burnham just before HW, go alongside the staithe, enjoy a pint in The Hero and put to sea again before the tide is away. The kayaker or dinghy enthusiast is also well served here and the sailing club welcoming. No jet skis or water-skiing though.

Without doubt, these harbourside villages of North Norfolk are a delight, but for those who have voyaged from further afield, very possibly in deeper draught boats, they are perhaps best reached from landward. With the all tide mooring options now available in King's Lynn and Wells-next-the-Sea, coupled with the charming coastal bus service, there is scope to visit these havens without the ramifications of being high and dry and then re-floating.

Burnham Overy Harbour is managed by a charitable trust and the Harbour Warden is a source of local knowledge.

For advice in advance of a visit, contact via www.burnhamoveryharbour.com

Approaches

Aim for fair weather with offshore winds. Winds with any north in them, or even the residual swell as a result, can make entry untenable. Overfalls can occur here.

If planning to enter Burnham, a coasting approach from the east is most likely, as the tide will then be favourable. If Wells is your last port and you leave there sufficiently before HW, then entry to Burnham on the same tide is possible. Generally, entry should be HW +/-2hrs given a draught of no more than 1.5m. On neap tides closer to HW is preferable. The ebb tide can flow with some purpose.

Approach is over Holkham Bay, but from further offshore, Bridgirdle PHM Fl.R 2.5s is a sensible offing waypoint to avoid the Bridgirdle shoal. See plan page 14.

Entry is between Gun Hill and the eastern end of Scolt Head Island, approximately in position 52°59'·06N 000°46'·15E, but neither the course of the channel nor the point of entry are constant. Gun Hill is conspicuous.

Visual references for the point of entry are the church towers of Burnham Overy and Burnham Market.

The scoured channel across the inter-tidal flats is marked with five small, unlit lateral buoys leading to the river proper between Gun Hill and the east end of Scolt Head.

Entry and moorings

Once inside what passes for the headlands, the course of the river errs first to port then sweeps to starboard around the sea bank and the higher, agricultural land on the port hand. It is not until you are further in that moored boats provide more of an indication as to the course of the river.

At every step, caution is the watchword, as from time to time there are stone groynes to combat erosion, perpendicular to the stream. These cover as the tide floods.

Once at the staithe, where to moor will depend on intentions and the advice from the Harbour Warden.

Facilities and visitor information

The village is as charming as any on this coast and the buildings, with their mix of brick and flint, provide an attractive backdrop.

Independent shops are nearby. The Burnhams are well used to visitors as one would expect, and around high tide times, activity increases, especially on the small boat scene.

If the opportunity exists for a visit of longer duration than the tide allows, bracing walks are here to be enjoyed and a ferry from the staithe takes passengers to Scolt Head Island, the National Nature Reserve owned by the National Trust and managed by Natural England. It is rich in flora and fauna on its shingle, dune and saltmarsh habitats.

Two miles inland is Burnham Thorpe, noted as the birthplace of Horatio Nelson and where his father was the rector of All Saints' Church. Given the slightest interest in the history of Nelson, a visit to the church is a visceral connection. With a complete absence of interpretation panels, audio guides and buttons to press, the church is one Nelson would recognise and, unless things have changed dramatically, a kindly church warden may conduct a short tour and show some artifacts directly attributable to the man himself. Your imagination will do the rest. And then there's the nearby hostelry bearing his name. It's a great day out.

For places to visit in and around Burnham Overy and information on making the most of a visit, look at:

www.scoltheadisland.co.uk
www.burnhamoveryboathouse.co.uk
www.overstaithesc.org.uk
www.holkham.co.uk

Smack Primrose in Overy Creek
Ash Faire-Ring

Approaching the Staithe at high water
Ash Faire-Ring

Final reach before the Staithe

Brancaster Staithe

Brancaster Staithe is another of the attractive drying harbours on the North Norfolk coast, though not a ready option for those with deeper draughted boats or those unable to take the ground.

Beautiful beaches, Scolt Head Island, a National Nature Reserve, salt marshes and bird and wild life typify this gem lying on the Norfolk Coastal Path between Hunstanton and Wells-next-the-Sea.

For the boating visitor, launching from the hard and going afloat over a high tide is the most frequently employed option. Kayakers, dinghy sailors, sail boarders and even water skiers are active here but visiting craft should contact the harbour office for advice. The summer months are especially busy and if you expect to simply turn up, launch and sail, you will risk disappointment. There are competing interests, and harbour bye-laws and codes of practice apply. There is also a charge, albeit modest.

For the visitor from seaward, how one intends to use Brancaster Harbour will influence planning. For example, a catamaran may well enjoy a night inside Scolt Head, dried out on the sand, which would entail only nosing in for a few cables and tucking into Norton Creek. But if Brancaster night life is your objective you will need to find the course of the channel into Mow Creek and up to the staithe.

Potential hazards, apart from unintended grounding, are an ebb which runs hard, moored craft, and the intensity of small boat activity, such as dinghy racing and water skiing, over HW. There are also mussel beds where anchoring is forbidden as well as designated 'no landing zones' at certain times of year to avoid disturbing nesting birds.

The National Trust is the harbour authority. The Harbourmaster can be contacted on ☏ +44 7810 850334 and a 'must' is to download the Brancaster Harbour guide from www.nationaltrust.org.uk/brancaster-estate/brancaster-staithe-harbour

Approaches

Of most importance, as with the entire coast here, is an assessment of the viability of the harbour when the wind is, or has been, in the NW to NE quadrant.

From the east, timings can be tricky. But when conditions are benign, approach from the west on a favourable rising tide via the Sledway from the Woolpack PHM Fl.R. 10s,

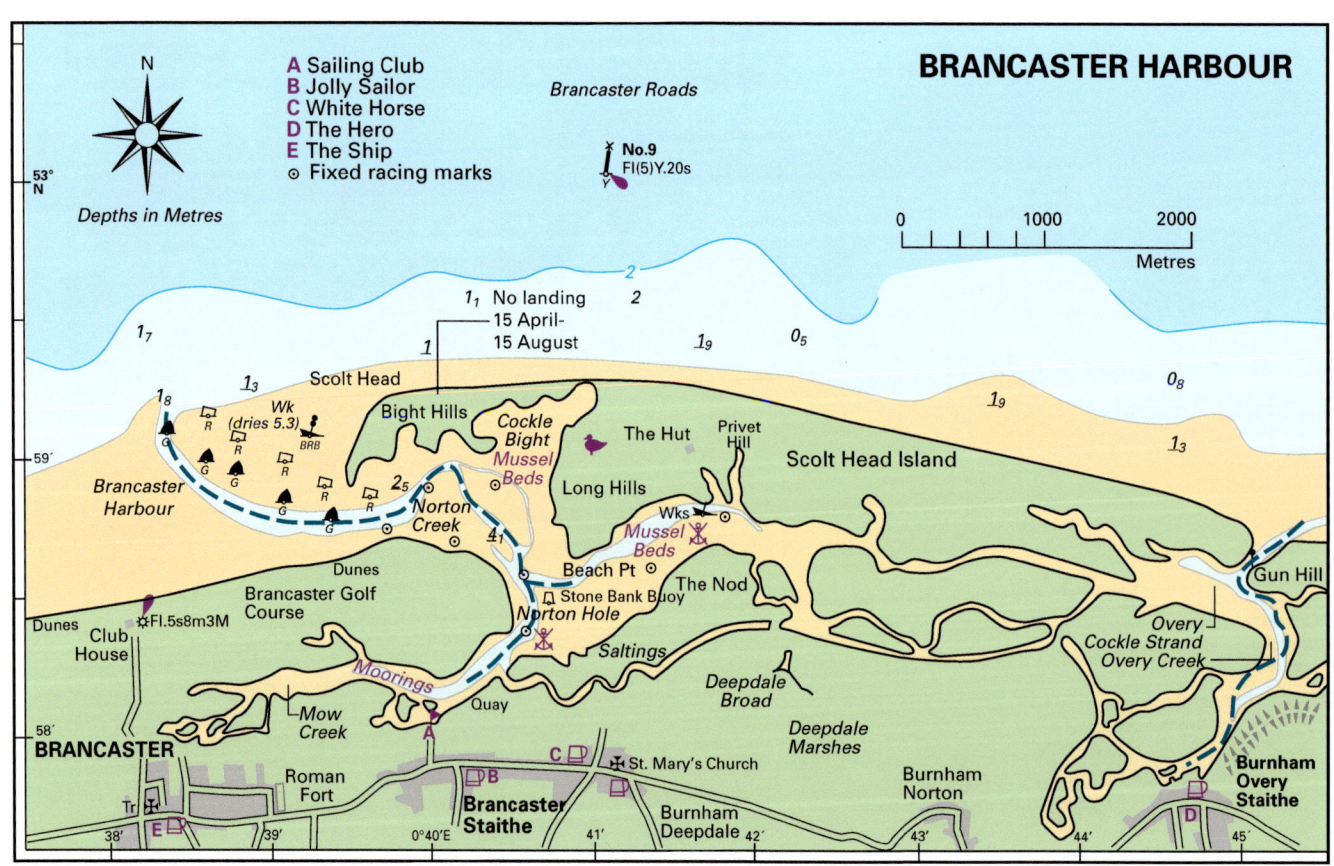

Brancaster Staithe

or further inshore inside Middle Bank and Gore Middle. The channel through The Bays was surveyed in 2020 and is reflected in the latest charts.

From the Woolpack, a course of 126° for 5M leads into Brancaster Bay and the visual, landward references are a conspicuous communications towers and, closer in, the wreck exposed at LW immediately to the west of Scolt Head. Charted notionally as an IDM (BRB) but unlit, in fact it has three vertical black balls to the midships section of the vessel's remains. The fo'c'sle and the aft superstructure survive but do not bear topmarks, so all best given a wide berth. The wreck's charted position is 52°59'·13N 000°39'·27E.

Entry

The scoured channel to follow inward is approximately 0.4M to the west. This channel is not constant, but is delineated by a series of lit buoys running inside the line of Scolt Head. At the time of writing there were five pairs of buoys.

During the sailing season, the Brancaster Staithe Sailing Club set racing marks and you will encounter these as the channel swings seaward before forming a bight known as Norton Creek. Follow the creek until it turns

Useful information – Brancaster

Fairway buoy Entrance runs from 4 cables west of a wreck, most of which covers. Charted position of Isolated Danger Mark is 52°59'·14N 000°39'·29E. Note also minor shore beacon Fl. 5s. 8m3M and golf clubhouse.

Buoyed channel Some lit buoys laid in pairs lead to largely unmarked inner reaches.

Moorings Many laid moorings but anchoring an option with advice. In some areas anchoring is forbidden. All moorings dry.

Contacts Harbourmaster
☏ +44 7810 850334
Harbour Authority National Trust
www.nationaltrust.org.uk/brancaster-estate/brancaster-staithe-harbour

VHF Port Working Channel No dedicated channel.

Tidal predictions based on Wells.

Hazards Offshore winds can render entry unviable. Entry according to draught and height of tide close to local HW. Ebb runs strongly.

Charts Admiralty 108 Imray Y9

Wreck west of Scolt Head off Brancaster Harbour entrance

approximately southwards at Stone Bank Buoy where the Norton Creek turns to port and Mow Creek continues to the south then southwest towards the Staithe. Note that Stone Bank buoy is so named for a reason and should be left 30m to port, using the racing marks as a guide.

Be aware that an 8kt speed limit applies within the harbour area between May and September. This reduces to 6kts inward of Stone Bank buoy.

Head approximately southwest past many local boats moored here, towards the Staithe, the slipway, the sailing club and the Dial House, the National Trust building.

Moorings

Anchoring is best agreed with the Harbourmaster. There are many boats on swinging moorings to avoid and the mussel lays are assiduously protected. Far preferable is to pick up a vacant mooring as advised by the Harbourmaster. Bear in the mind the strong ebb, especially towards the harbour entrance. If anchoring away from the madding crowd, make sure that your anchor is well set.

Facilities and visitor information

Brancaster Staithe is part of a string of villages on this stretch of the coast road which include Brancaster to the west, and Burnham Deepdale and Burnham Norton to the east. Slightly inland is Burnham Market. Between them all they will cope with most needs, including marine supplies from E.F. Snelling & Son, an old established local business which caters, in the main, for the needs of the day boat sailor.

Most culinary tastes, budgets and dress codes are accommodated within easy walking

Brancaster Staithe Sailing Club

Moorings off Brancaster Staithe. Better with the tide in

distance and, as one would expect, locally caught seafood features strongly. The Brancaster Staithe Sailing Club is comfortably housed, has good, modern facilities and welcomes visiting members of other clubs.

Alternative activities aimed at the land based visitor are in abundance. The coastal bus service runs to Wells and Cromer to the east and Hunstanton and King's Lynn to the west. Go to www.visitwestnorfolk.com and www.visitnorthnorfolk.co.uk for more details.

Local information – www.brancasterstaithe.co.uk
Brancaster Staithe Sailing Club – www.bssc.net
Brancaster Staithe Ski Boat Owners' Club – www.bssboc.org.uk
Brancaster Harbour Users Association – ☏ +44 1485 576029
National Nature Reserve – www.scoltheadisland.co.uk

Thornham

Devotees of the book *The Riddle of the Sands* will be familiar with the practice of one of the central characters, Davies, of drying his boat out on some isolated sand, then roaming as far as the low water period allowed to take bearings which, come the time the sands were covered again, would enable him to navigate the creeks and swatchways, now rendered invisible. Spirited stuff.

Should the mariner visiting North Norfolk havens, and only then in a craft which can take the ground, feel the inclination to nose into Thornham, emulating Davies would be the recommendation.

This is not to speak ill of Thornham, one of the prettiest of a host of pretty options. But save for launching a kayak by the coal barn and pottering around while the tide serves, this historic haven, busy in the 1800s with cargo across the quay, is better left to the initiated.

Some local fishing boats still regard it as a home port but lack of permanent aids to navigation, and sands which tend towards the uncooperative, lead to it being omitted from this pilot.

Though speaking of the Thornham coal barn, an industrial archaeological gem, if the reader has the relevant interest why not join the many who have this photographic icon in their portfolio? Reason to visit. And there's always The Lifeboat, The Chequers and the Thornham Deli.

Photogenic Thornham coal barn
Gary Garford

Norfolk, The Wash and Humber

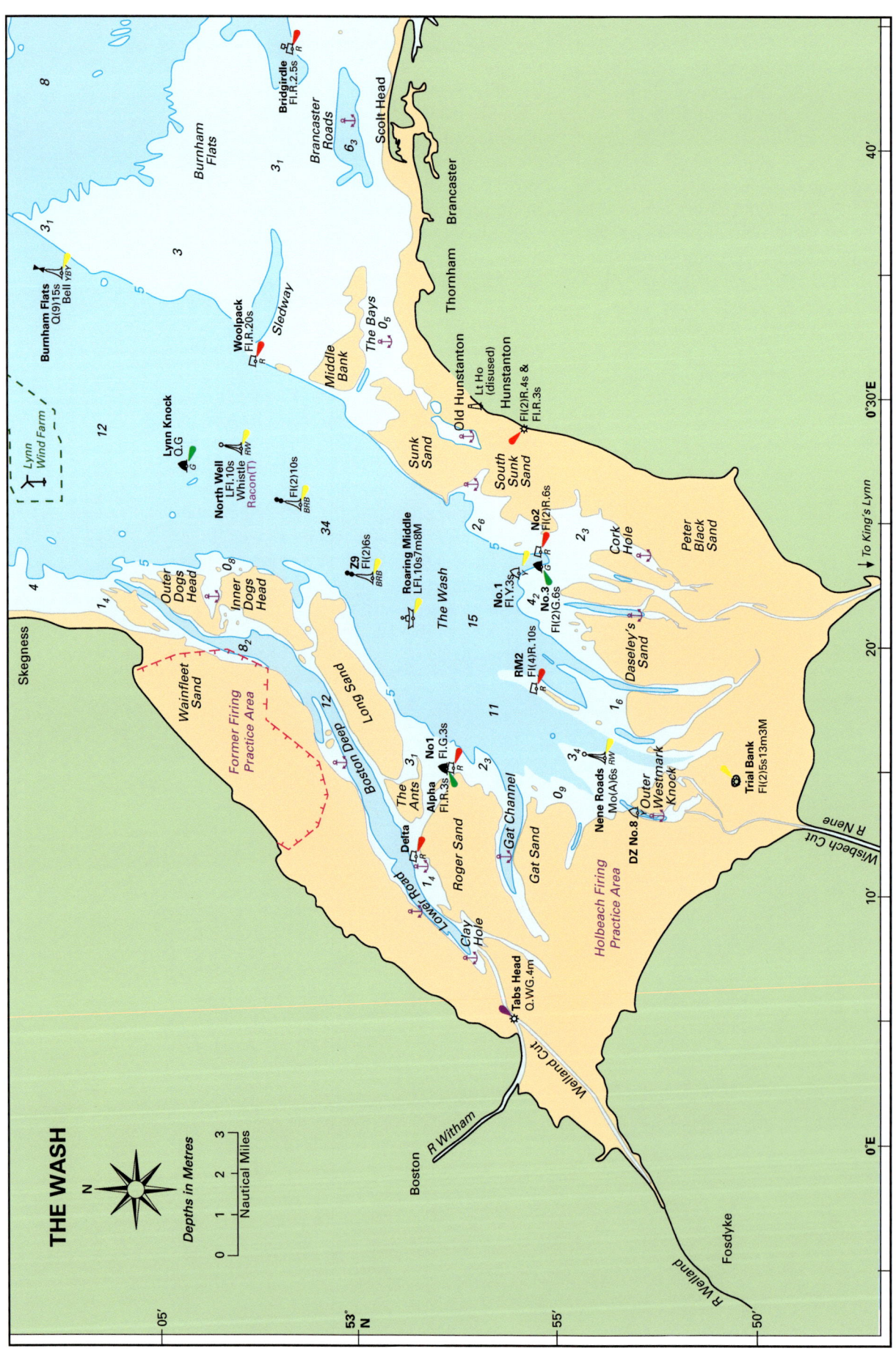

THE WASH

The Wash and its approaches have, over time, acquired a somewhat tarnished reputation with visiting sailors. A study of the relevant charts however, while clearly showing many areas requiring caution, also reveals sufficient deep water for safe navigation without undue concern. The commercial ports of King's Lynn, Boston, Wisbech and Sutton Bridge, with their regular flow of short sea trading vessels, bear witness to there being draught enough for the average cruising yacht. Some fifty or more inshore fishing boats work out of Boston and King's Lynn.

And because of these ports, buoyage is extensive, inshore surveys frequent and the topical data promulgated on the respective harbour authorities' web pages for the benefit of all.

The Wash embayment of some 200 square miles, from Gibraltar Point to the northwest and Gore Point to the southeast is, with the exception of the varied colours of the Hunstanton cliffs, low lying and lacking in landward feature. The exceptions, given clear visibility, are the disused lighthouse and the water tower in Hunstanton, the RAF Holbeach firing range control tower, St. Botolph's Church, Boston, known as the Boston Stump, and Trial Bank close to the mouth of the River Nene.

Trial Bank looking east. But a conspicuous profile from any viewpoint

Anchorages in The Wash (see plans on pages 30, 35, 48)

⚓ Gat Channel	⊕ 52°56'·0N 00°12'·8E
⚓ Outer Westmark Knock	⊕ 52°52'·7N 00°13'·2E
⚓ Delta	⊕ 52°58'·4N 00°11'·0E
⚓ Lower Road	⊕ 52°58'·0N 00°08'·8E
⚓ Boston Deep	⊕ 53°00'·5N 00°15'·2E
⚓ Clay Hole	⊕ 52°57'·1N 00°07'·4E
⚓ Outer Dogs Head	⊕ 53°03'·8N 00°22'·3E
⚓ The Bays	⊕ 52°59'·7N 00°32'·0E
⚓ Holkham Bay	⊕ 52°59'·6N 00°48'·0E
⚓ Old Hunstanton	⊕ 52°57'·6N 00°28'·3E
⚓ Daseley's Sled	⊕ 52°53'·7N 00°21'·4E
⚓ Cork Hole	⊕ 52°53'·2N 00°23'·9E
⚓ South Sunk Sand	⊕ 52°57'·4N 00°26'·0E

Anchoring positions are approximate. While marine traffic around The Wash is not dense, displaying day shapes and anchor lights as appropriate is highly recommended.

It is true that features on the low-lying coasts are more difficult to identify from a distance than, for example, a high headland with a lighthouse, but a little time devoted to a plan, to include safe anchorages in case of need, will ensure a safe passage and timely arrival. A chart plotter as a navigational aid should inspire confidence when negotiating the inter-tidal channels.

Fed by four principal rivers; The Witham, Welland, Nene and Great Ouse, the port towns which sit on them have had sea trading significance since Roman times. All the rivers, to a greater or lesser extent, offer links to an extensive inland waterway network. If your vessel has suitable air draught, the cities of Lincoln, Peterborough, Ely and Cambridge are within reach.

The Wash is a significant habitat for migrating birds and home to the UK's largest common seal population. The tidal flows enable shellfish to breed including shrimp, cockles and mussels.

Many statutory, environmental and ecological protections are in place and, in 1996, The Wash and North Norfolk coast were designated a European Marine Site.

In 1216, King John is said to have lost much of his treasure as a result of an ill-advised low tide crossing with his baggage train and, to this day, speculative searches continue.

More topically and considered a local spectator sport, the RAF air weapons training range at the southern extreme plays host to all NATO air forces who, using practice ordnance (which nevertheless can be spectacular), train here regularly. The targets, characterised by their bright orange colour, can be seen clearly on the inter tidal area inside the danger zone yellow special marks.

The Wainfleet range towards Gibraltar Point, shown on older charts and still designated by DZ buoys, was decommissioned in 2010.

River Nene East Lighthouse

The Wash

The Fens Waterways Link

Having touched on the topic of regeneration, it is worth noting this particular project as an illustration of the continued commitment to marine tourism within the eastern region.

Billed as the most significant waterways development in the UK for two centuries, the project aims, through the use of 240km of new and existing watercourses to link the cathedral cities of Lincoln, Peterborough and Ely as well as Cambridge and beyond.

Planned in 2004 and reckoned to require 15-20 years to complete at a cost of £130m, this ambitious plan has at least seen its initial phase opened with the rebuilt Black Sluice Lock in Boston opening up 35km of navigation, previously closed for fifty years.

But as with much that was expected during the last decade or more, timescales stretch and budgets balloon and given the inevitable multi-agency involvement, the term 'perfect storm' springs to mind. Work nonetheless progresses and the will remains.

As can be seen from the project map, The Wash is integral to local waterway links, a factor which features highly in the narrowboat fraternity's 'must do' list of passages. While narrowboats were hardly designed for seagoing, a boating season never passes without some of the more adventurous owners; usually in convoy, venturing down the tidal reaches of the Witham, Great Ouse or Nene, crossing The Wash to enter a different river, re-capturing the tranquillity of non-tidal cruising and the delights of new destinations.

To suggest this crossing is the 'Everest' of narrowboating might be overstating the case, but it is another example of what this region offers those with boats suitable for inland cruising, leading to the enjoyment of previously unconsidered opportunities.

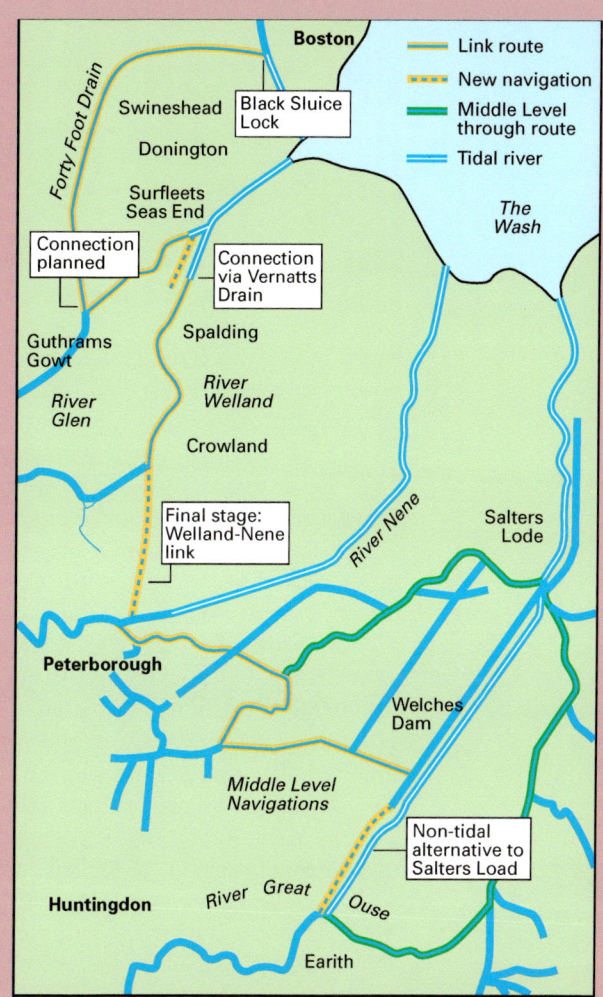

Narrowboats crossing The Wash

TIDAL HAVENS OF THE WASH

King's Lynn

Standing proud on the River Great Ouse King's Lynn was at one time rated England's most important port. When trade with Europe was dominant and the Hanseatic League all powerful, King's Lynn was crucial to the country's prosperity. It was not until the growth of west coast ports with the opening up of the Americas, followed by the Industrial Revolution, that this importance waned.

All things being relative, there remained much coastal traffic and, until the advent of the railways at least, King's Lynn continued, economically, to face the sea. Regional agriculture was served by the port and commercial fishing featured strongly. Thankfully for the modern visitor, Blubberhouse Creek is no more nor is there any olfactory evidence of the whaling trade.

In the main, river traffic is still commercial, to and from the enclosed, locked docks which were developed in the mid 19th century. More recently, however, and through the initiative of the local council, an all-tide landing for small, leisure craft has been built on the east bank, close to the old town itself. Already this has proved popular with visitors from both seaward and upstream, where the non-tidal reaches of the river lead at least to the cathedral city of Ely and on to Cambridge. For this prospect, nothing better than Imray's title 'The River Great Ouse and its tributaries' by Chris Howes.

The advent of this 'Town Quay,' created another strategic location for leisure boating in the region, making the greater Wash area a viable place to visit and cruise.

Approaches

It is easy to think of the sands of the intertidal areas here as constantly moving but that is perhaps, to overstate the case. While spot depths change from time to time, these are picked up by the harbour authorities' regular surveys and for the most part, small alterations to the positions of navigation marks suffice. Occasionally however, channels break through and divert and although this is a gradual process, it can necessitate more major changes. And the buoyed approach channel to King's Lynn is no exception. Keep abreast of any changes by consulting the harbour authority website (see 'Useful information' over page).

From along the North Norfolk coast, the PHM Woolpack Fl R 10s then 235° for 7M will bring up Roaring Middle LFl 10s before altering to approximately 156° for 3M towards Bulldog Channel, the final, buoyed approach route.

From the north, enter The Wash via North Well RW LFl 10s in position 53°03'·01N 000°27'·89 E, then by a course of 223° to RW Roaring Middle and towards the Bulldog Channel as above. In either case, on a rising tide but do not enter the final, buoyed approach channel before HW –3hrs.

The Norfolk coasting passage can be shortened slightly, particularly if the wind has been unfavourably from ahead and closer in could facilitate bearing away a little. The inshore line is through The Bays between Gore Point and Middle Bank. Although unbuoyed, this channel was surveyed in 2020 and, given sufficient height of tide, is an option.

The Bays too offers a sheltered anchorage if the wind has south in it or, even if not, under the lee of Middle Bank. The anchorage is charted and the holding, mainly in sand, is good.

King's Lynn pontoon
King's Lynn & West Norfolk BC

Norfolk, The Wash and Humber

> **Useful information – River Great Ouse for King's Lynn**
>
> **Fairway buoy** No.1 Fl. Y 3s 52°56'·00N 00°23'·00E
>
> **Buoyed channel** See local chartlet from harbour authority for all AtoN positions.
>
> **Moorings** enquiries to Borough Council of King's Lynn & West Norfolk NOT the harbour authority. Contact via www.sailthewash.co.uk
>
> **Contacts**
> *Harbour Authority* King's Lynn Conservancy Board. (KLCB) www.kingslynnport.co.uk
>
> **VHF Port Working Channel** 14
>
> **Tidal predictions based on** Bull Dog tide gauge and King's Lynn Dock Sill. See KLCB website.
>
> **Charts** Admiralty 1200 and Imray Y9

Staying close in past Hunstanton is also viable as the 2020 survey included this area too. Keeping inside Sunk Sand gives not only a good view of Hunstanton and Old Hunstanton but an anchorage here is possible in a small well with charted depth of 2.8m. If conditions allow, this could make for a pleasant pause.

A two-point fix when the disused lighthouse bears 084° and the water tower 126° is the time for a wheel over to steer just north of west out into The Wash proper. From here, Bulldog Channel is under 3M.

The King's Lynn fairway buoy equivalent is a yellow special mark No.1 Fl Y 3s in position 52°56'·00N 000°23'·00E. Thereafter, a course made good of 174° brings up first the SHM (No.3) and PHM (No.2), then SHM No.5 and PHM No.4, both laid as pairs to guide into the Bulldog Channel proper. The course from here to Lynn Cut is essentially southwards but with periodic, minor deviations.

Note that on the UKHO and Imray charts, because of scale, not all the channel marks are shown. For the benefit of a local chartlet which also takes account of topical buoy movements, consult the King's Lynn Conservancy Board (KLCB) website www.kingslynnport.co.uk, where real time tide data can also be found.

In speaking of the harbour authority, it is worth noting that the visitor pontoon in King's Lynn is not their responsibility. While they are always prepared, at reasonable times, to advise over safe passage making, and while they prefer those in command of small craft to monitor the port working channel VHF 14 to keep abreast of commercial ship movements, there is no 24 hr VTS nor an on-demand source of local information, and they do not control berthing arrangements at the pontoon. For clarification over shipping movements, call 'Lynn Pilots' on VHF 14 from HW -2hrs.

As suggested elsewhere in this pilot, at the end of a long and testing passage and bound for a Wash port, there is a natural desire to be alongside as soon as possible. But there are two reasons at least to stick to a seamanlike plan. One concerns rate of tidal flow, particularly in the narrower rivers. Arriving amongst moorings with the tide running up strongly can be challenging. The other, of

The varied colours of the Hunstanton cliffs and the prominent disused lighthouse

course, is having sufficient height of tide once within an approach channel where charted depths begin to vary and reduce.

Decisions over killing time will depend on a variety of factors and if the need is to lose less than an hour or so then perhaps heaving to will suffice. But it would not be unusual, after a long passage, to be entering The Wash around LW, when three hours or more has to elapse before it's safe to begin a final approach within a channel. Time enough to anchor and put the kettle on.

So, where to anchor for King's Lynn? Options further out have been covered, but there is another closer in which can have the advantage of more shelter. Of greatest importance is not anchoring in buoyed channels, but with this proviso, NW of the SHM No.5 in the lee of Old Bell Middle can do the trick, depending on draught. Once committed in Bulldog Channel however, there is little other possibility.

Of course, if there are no ship movements, anchoring will unlikely embarrass anyone so by maintaining an awareness and with a readiness to weigh, all should be well.

Entry

To proceed up Bulldog Channel is not recommended until HW -3.5hrs at the earliest, and only then if the rise of tide is your vessel's draught +1m. In approximate terms the flood here is of 4hrs duration once it starts to rise, but various factors can impinge. Length of passage once in the Sled is over 10M. Treat the start of your passage from here as a VHF reporting point to 'Lynn Port' on VHF 14.

Be aware that from HW -2hrs, commercial vessels could be on passage inward from the No.1 buoy. Radio traffic on VHF 14 will raise awareness as will pilot boat activity. Ships could be outward too and these aim to be clear of Bulldog Channel by HW +1hr. In all cases, ships will be constrained by their draught and can navigate only in the buoyed channels.

The channel throughout its length is well buoyed and straightforward and the direction is, for the most part, southward to the West Stones NCM, where a training wall to the west of the channel runs to the river mouth. 1M further on at No.26 PHM, the channel takes a small turn to east of south and this is then the general direction as far as the visitor pontoon off the town. From East Stones PHM the training wall to the west is joined by a similar structure to the east. As the river mouth opens, visual references are tall pylons to each bank and two wind turbines to the east bank.

As you enter the river, the West Bank Fl.Y 2s is another VHF reporting point. Distance to run is now approximately 2.5M. From here, with the exception of Low Cut Beacon QR, there are no lit aids to navigation.

Always worth noting in the rivers of The Wash is speed over the ground when the tide's in your favour. A quick look at the bank, as opposed to dead ahead, can sometimes surprise.

If there is commercial traffic, this can be encountered from either or both directions now. Under the pylons is another reporting point to 'Lynn Docks' who will advise over ship movements.

Ships manoeuvring to enter the dock or ships leaving will, at some point, be at 90° to the stream and therefore blocking the channel temporarily before proceeding. Be prepared to hold station and be guided by port control. This is good reason to appreciate speed over the ground in case you need to turn to stem the tide while waiting.

Above the dock entrance and to the east side is Fisher Fleet, an inlet used by the many commercial fishing vessels operating from King's Lynn. Do not enter the fleet. There is no leisure mooring provision there.

The town opens up on the east bank and St. Nicholas' Chapel spire is visible, a day mark for centuries. A small passenger ferry operates from bank to bank, except on Sundays. Powerboats should reduce speed, and therefore wash, accordingly.

Roaring Middle Light Float The principal wash waypoint

King's Lynn No1 buoy, the Fairway equivalent

King's Lynn Visitor pontoon after its upgrade in 2021. Seen from downstream

King's Lynn quayside at low water looking north

Moorings

The only viable moorings are to the visitor pontoons. These now stand out clearly off the east bank, towards the south end of the built quay. Do not be tempted to secure to the quayside. The bed here dries and is not accommodating and the quay south of the pontoon is a commercial ship lay-by berth, which could be required at any time.

Further on is Boal Quay, used by some fishing vessels but not somewhere for leisure craft to secure.

Depths vary at the visitor pontoons according to berth and the local council, the operator of the moorings, will allocate berths depending on draught. They prefer to offer 1.5m as the maximum draught they can accommodate but they tend towards the cautious in this respect. Depending on height of tide at LW, there can be 2.5m+ on some berths. When making a booking, this is a conversation to have.

Booking in advance is important. Do not assume availability, especially at the height of the season. A lack of fellow sailors heading inward from The Wash is not a guide to occupancy levels. The facility is very popular with motor vessels from inland and finding the pontoon packed with such would be more than an embarrassment given the lack of alternatives.

Booking a berth is either via the Sail The Wash website www.sailthewash.com or by telephone ☏ +44 1553 774297. Enquiries in advance by email to visitorpontoons@west-norfolk.gov.uk. At the time of writing, fees are £1.75/metre/day of 24 hours. Maximum stay, 7 days.

There are only a few swinging moorings in the river and they lie towards the west bank. These are either in private or harbour authority use and depth is limited over LW.

Facilities and visitor information

King's Lynn, once Bishop's Lynn until Henry VIII took an interest, is the largest settlement in the region. It can provide most, if not all, the visiting mariner could require. The success of its pontoon has already led to the upgrading and lengthening of the original. So, the good burghers of Lynn are on the case.

Yet to be provided, however, are shoreside facilities. The land is earmarked but, at the time of writing, showers and toilets are unavailable. However, immediately ashore of the pontoon are a number of licensed establishments, one a surviving Hanseatic League warehouse which,

King's Lynn

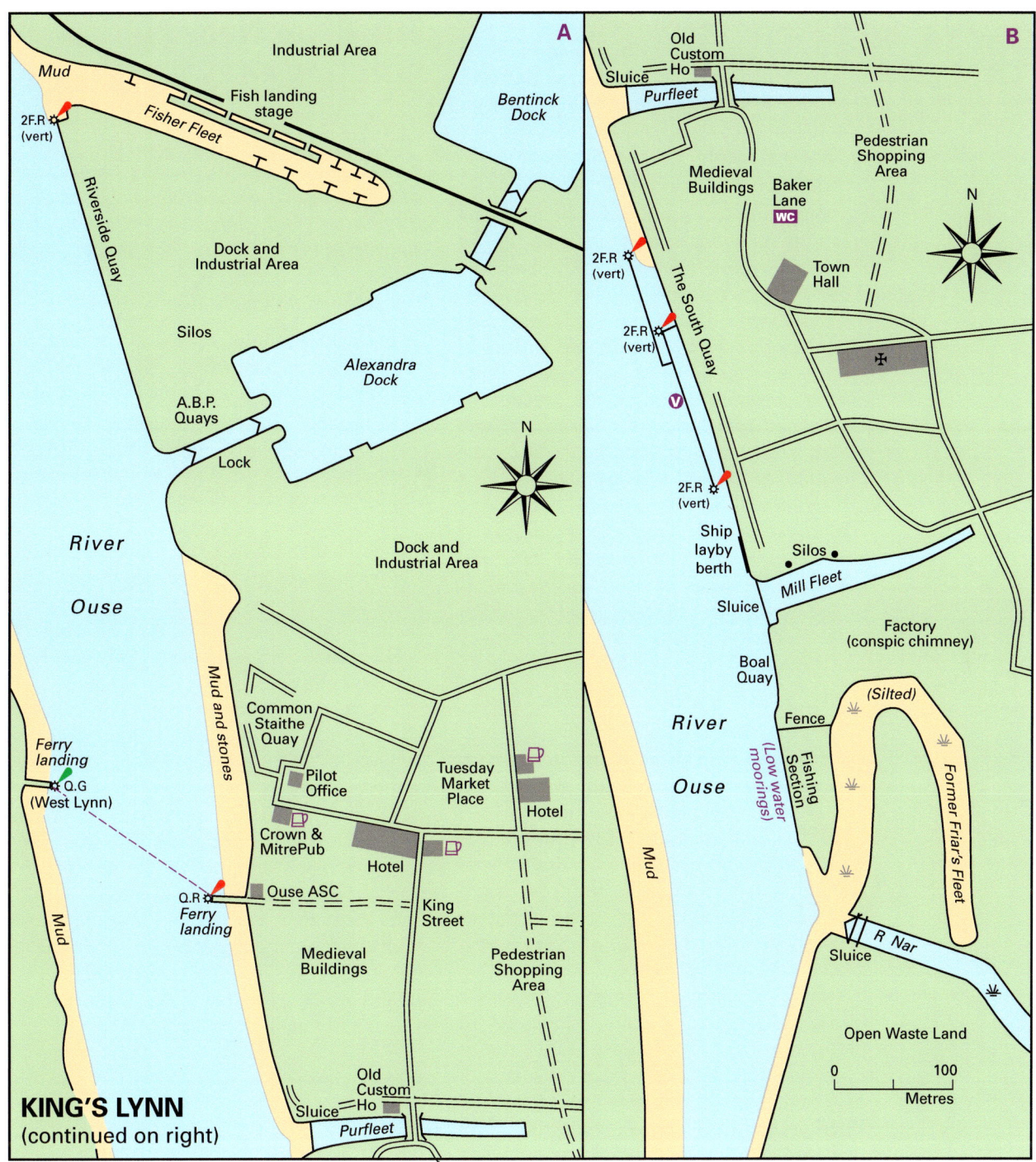

along with nearby Hanse House are the only two such buildings remaining in England. A modest investment across the bar here can prove convenient. Excellent public toilets are in Baker Lane 300m in the direction of the main market place. The Ouse Amateur Sailing Club, tucked away off King Street (see plan) welcomes visitors www.oasc.co.uk.

The buildings on and around South Quay give a taste of the architectural gems to be found in King's Lynn which make for, at the very least, an attractive run ashore. In particular, the Custom House, adjacent to The Purfleet, and Trinity Guildhall are worthy of more than a second glance.

The Purfleet, once the town's principal commercial anchorage, is now an enclosed basin, looked over by a statue to George Vancouver who, apart from sailing with James Cook's second and third voyages, undertook his own extensive exploration. A famous son of King's Lynn, Vancouver, of Dutch family origin, has his name immortalised around the world. So accurate was his surveying in the northwest Pacific, that his maps and charts remained the basis of navigation there until well into the 20th century. Not bad considering he died aged 40.

A man noted for his good relations with the indigenous peoples he met, he made some trenchant observations on the topic.

> *'I am extremely concerned to be compelled to state here, that many of the traders from the civilised world have not only pursued a line of conduct, diametrically opposite to the true principles of justice in their commercial dealings, but have fomented discords, and stirred up contentions, between the different tribes, in order to increase the demand for these destructive engines... They have been likewise eager to instruct the natives in the use of European arms of all descriptions; and have shewn by their own example, that they consider gain as the only object of pursuit; and whether this be acquired by fair and honourable means, or otherwise, so long as the advantage is secured, the manner how it is obtained seems to have been, with too many of them, but a very secondary consideration.'*

Plus ça change, plus c'est la même chose.

The local Maritime Trail, for which a written guide is available from the Tourist Information Office, will reward any visitor with even a passing interest in matters maritime.

All the usual stores and provisioning are within walking distance too. Restaurants abound, some overlooking the river. For a very warm welcome, the Ouse Amateur Sailing Club in Ferry Lane, off King Street, can be a colourful diversion.

King's Lynn is well connected by public transport and trains run frequently to destinations throughout East Anglia and to London. A regular bus service runs west to east (and vice versa) between termini in Peterborough and Norwich, with connections there to Lowestoft.

A more local service, previously The Coast Hopper, does exactly that along the scenic North Norfolk coast, opening up the delights of its many villages and small towns, and indeed tidal harbours, which those cruising in deeper draught boats would otherwise not enjoy. No apology here for suggesting leaving the boat in King's Lynn for a day, or even longer, and taking in, for example, Nelson's birth place.

Only 6 miles from King's Lynn is Sandringham House with its gardens and courtyard (bus No.35 from the bus station).

The River Nene to Sutton Bridge & Wisbech

'Too early for the tide into the river, I nonetheless allowed the start of the flood to ease me towards the waiting anchorage. On the Outer Gat Sand, a seal and pup considered me idly and a flock of gulls which earlier, had been engaged in vigorous competition, now hove to out of curiosity.'

The Nene, pronounced 'Neen' or 'Nenn', depending on which stretch one lives by, rises near Northampton in England's Midlands and meanders over approximately 100 miles, 88 of which are navigable, through Cambridgeshire, flirts with Norfolk and finally enters The Wash amid low-lying Lincolnshire.

Tidal to the Dog-in-a-Doublet sea lock near the cathedral city of Peterborough, the principal interests for cruising folk are the facilities at Sutton Bridge and in Wisbech with both offering modern, fully serviced pontoon moorings.

The village of Sutton Bridge, 3M from the river mouth, is convenient as somewhere to lay over for a tide or to wait before proceeding south to Wisbech, 7M further on. Wisbech, a town with much attractive Georgian architecture and a long maritime history, lays claim as 'The Capital of the Fens.' Its yacht harbour is hard by the town centre.

As with other rivers of The Wash, for those with either the right craft or the inclination to adapt, the River Nene provides, ultimately, an inland water way link to the Grand Union Canal and much in between.

Approaches

See plan on page 35.

The River Nene is no exception in this region in being best tackled from half tide rising. Depending on passage timings, however, there exists the scope for being in shoal waters too early. Under these circumstances, rather than stooge around further out, if conditions are sufficiently benign, the Outer Westmark Knock all tide anchorage in the vicinity of DZ No.9 is a sensible option. Here there is ample deep water. (See photograph). Shape a course of approximately 220° up the Wisbech channel from the Nene Roads SWM, taking care to err towards yellow special mark DZ No.8 to avoid cutting the corner of the Outer

The River Nene

The Nene opens up past the East Lighthouse but stay in the buoyed channel

Westmark Knock sand. The most favourable anchorage is east of DZ No.9 where deep water is to be found even over LW springs. Avoid being west of this cardinal mark where a wreck lies which covers.

Come predicted HW – 3, departure for the river can be taken by steering a reciprocal course towards Nene Roads then following the buoyed channel from East Knock ECM. Alternatively, and if the wind direction better suits, proceed generally southwards from the anchorage to join the buoyed approach channel in the vicinity of SHM No.7. Using the western extreme of Trial Bank as a transit can serve here. Course to steer is approximately 155°.

If Wisbech is the object of the passage, unless one's air draught is small, it will be necessary to arrange for the bridge at Sutton Bridge to open. At the time of writing, 24 hours notice is required, even though, in theory, it should be available on demand. Make early contact with the bridge keeper. See 'Useful information' page 42.

Buoyage of the entire approach channel can be obtained on a local chartlet via the harbour authority website www.fenland.gov.uk or through prior contact with the harbour office. As buoy positions change from time to time, having this chartlet to hand is recommended as not all buoyage is shown on published charts, given their reduced scale.

Entry

Once in the main, buoyed approach channel, the remaining passage into the river is straightforward and, as the river opens up, the East and West Lighthouses are convenient daymarks. These structures, which once marked the outermost end of the man-made channel, have never actually functioned as lighthouses, as the channel's length was extended seaward from where they stand. However, the lighthouse owners are given to burning a light in their topmost windows, which is friendly to say the least.

Care should be exercised, on sighting the river ahead, to leave SHMs Dale and Big Annie as intended and not cut the corner, which is shoal. All is now clear to Sutton Bridge, 3M to the south.

It should be remembered that both Sutton Bridge and Wisbech remain busy commercial ports in the coastal and short sea trade. Wisbech accepts vessels up to 83m LOA and Sutton Bridge, given less tidal and other constraint, can accommodate ships over 100m LOA. Ship movements are more likely over spring tides and all such vessels are subject to local pilotage. Those in charge of small craft should not hesitate to make contact with pilots or the pilot cutter on VHF 09 for guidance. See 'Useful information' page 42.

River Nene fairway buoy, Nene Roads SWM

Anchorage at DZ No.9 Tide Gauge looking SE by S towards Trial Bank

Norfolk, The Wash and Humber

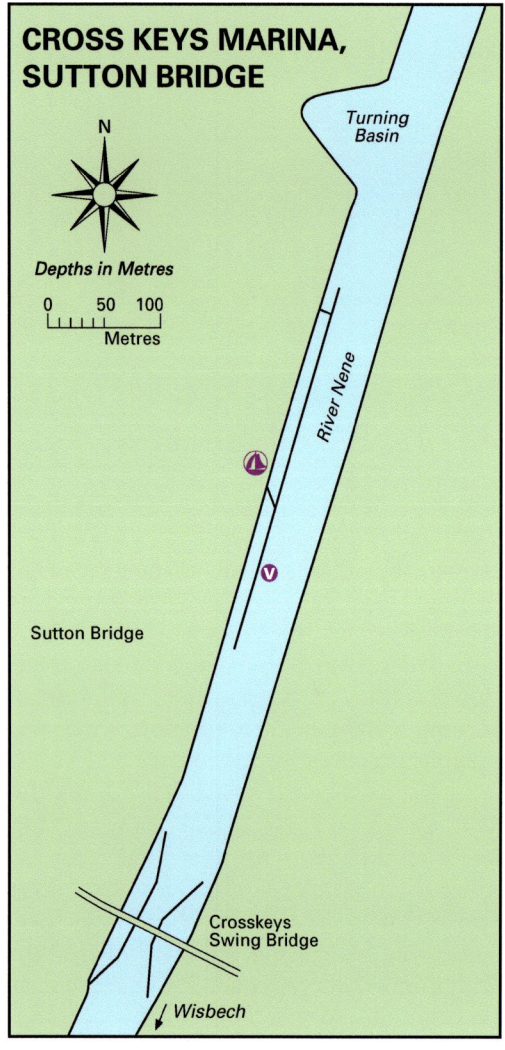

Useful information – River Nene for Sutton Bridge and Wisbech

Fairway buoy Nene Roads SWM Mo(A)6s. 52°52'·85N 000° 15'·47E

Buoyed channel See local chartlet from harbour authority for all channel marker positions.

Moorings Cross Keys Marina, Sutton Bridge and Wisbech Yacht Harbour (above bridge).

Contacts ℡ +44 1945 588059 for all marina mooring enquiries.
Harbour Authority Nene Ports Authority (Fenland District Council) www.fenland.gov.uk

VHF Port Working Channel 09.

Tidal predictions based on Wisbech Cut (river mouth) and Port Sutton Bridge.

Bridge Keeper Cross Keys Swing Bridge 24 hours notice required. ℡ +44 1406 350364 VHF 09.

Charts Admiralty 1200. Imray Y9

Sutton Bridge Port, where there be ships

Cross Keys Marina, Sutton Bridge

Situated upstream of the port and immediately below Cross Keys Swing Bridge, a glorious Victorian edifice which originally carried not only road but rail traffic across the river, is Cross Keys Marina, hard by the village itself.

Approach

Careful note needs to be taken as to the rate and direction of tidal flow when preparing to come alongside. On springs, tides can exceed 6 knots through Sutton Bridge and on occasions there is little or no stand. So if approach is on the flood, mariners are warned to turn early in the tideway *and before the moorings are reached*, allowing the tide to make the sternway with control being maintained by motoring ahead as necessary. This is how commercial ships do it so why not small craft?

On that note, commercial vessels bound for Sutton Bridge are very likely to make passage from the river mouth stern first. So if a seaward pointing ship is encountered in the river, do not assume it is heading to sea.

Moorings

The modern, fully serviced pontoons offer permanent moorings as well as short stay berths for visitors, who should moor as near as possible to the access ramp. On arrival, contact the harbour authority on VHF 09 or by telephone on the numbers displayed. See 'Useful information'. There are charges relating to visitors in the tariff but for an occasional overnight stay there is a good chance of no charge being made.

Cross Keys Marina, Sutton Bridge

Facilities

The village of Sutton Bridge, within easy walking distance of its moorings, provides much that is required from a short stay. There is a well stocked shop, take away restaurants, fish and chips, and the Riverside Bar and Restaurant. This establishment is also a guest house and, until showers and toilets are provided at the marina, is the only likely, local source of such facilities. There is a good hardware and tool shop and while no pure chandlery lines are stocked, many basic items can be found for purposes of repairs.

Useful information

19th century Sutton Bridge was but a few cottages and farm houses but its location was significant as an historic river crossing place when the area was marshland and the track between Lincolnshire and Norfolk was passable only at low water. Crossing was at some risk owing to shifting, running silt and quicksands and safe passage across was not guaranteed.

The most notable loss, according to legend was King John's baggage train, including the crown jewels, in 1216, and many expensive attempts to locate this hoard have been made to no avail, over time since. Bridges were of course a logical progression and the existing swing bridge dates from 1897, being the third to serve the purpose.

The present port at Sutton Bridge was built in 1987 and all berths are in the river where ships take the ground at low water. Historically however, a locked dock was constructed and the first ship to use it entered in 1881. Sadly, and amid the grand opening festivities in June of that year, some of the adjacent land subsided and despite frantic efforts, the dock walls collapsed. Three ships fortunately got away, albeit with difficulty, but the scheme was abandoned. Some of the original concrete walls are now incorporated into the local golf course.

The Royal Air Force has a long association with Sutton Bridge where flying training and a gunnery school were pivotal, particularly in the war effort from 1939. RAF Holbeach nearby, remains active as a practice bombing range for RAF and NATO air forces and when in use, can provide much entertainment for boats on passage in and out of the River Nene.

For those wishing to stretch legs, or if equipped with two wheeled transport, a sojourn to the East Lighthouse can be worthwhile. Built in 1831, both lighthouses commemorated the opening of the Nene outfall cut, the river here being man made as part of the many drainage and reclamation schemes which account for much of local landscape.

The East Lighthouse is notable as having been occupied in the 1930s by the naturalist Sir Peter Scott and was featured in Paul Gallico's novel, *The Snow Goose – A Story of Dunkirk*. Scott formed a wildfowl nature reserve here which was forerunner to his world famous Slimbridge Wetland Centre in Gloucestershire. With the right weather, a walk along the sea bank nearby makes for perfect views across the beautiful, arguably unique fen land and seascape.

The fully serviced pontoons of Cross Keys Marina, Sutton Bridge

Norfolk, The Wash and Humber

Approaching Cross Keys Swing Bridge
Mark Ashley-Miller

Departure

A passage plan from Sutton Bridge will depend on your next objective. If to seaward, it is likely that you will want a full tide away. Times in the local tide tables are for Wisbech Cut, that is at the river mouth. It is advisable to push the last of the flood in order to get the full benefit on leaving the river confines.

If Wisbech is the next port of call, remember that HW there is 30 minutes after Wisbech Cut and slack water Wisbech can be an hour after that. While it is tempting to head upstream as soon as the flood begins, the downside is arriving in Wisbech with too much tide underneath than is ideal. More of that planning is covered in the next section, 'Moorings – Wisbech.'

Wisbech

While Sutton Bridge serves best for a 'stop over' before either returning to sea or continuing up river, Wisbech is worthy of including in a cruising itinerary for a host of reasons and for a longer stay too.

It could hardly be more sheltered, the all tide moorings are fully serviced and diesel is available at the fuel and black tank pump out berth. Gas can be bought nearby. The showers and toilets are close in the ultra modern harbour office building, The Boathouse, where there is also a laundry. Crab Marsh Boatyard has 75 tonne lift out capability and many marine trades are on hand or available, given a little notice. 24 hour CCTV monitors the berths and Wisbech is used by many for overwintering afloat. The low salinity and relatively fast fluvial flow make for few problems with marine growth below the waterline.

Approaches

Whether direct from sea or via a rest in Sutton Bridge, planning a passage to Wisbech must include arranging a bridge opening. Having said that, there is approximately 3.40m air draught clearance at MHWS which serves some smaller craft, subject to confirmation with the bridge keeper on VHF 09.

According to the founding Act which established the bridge, opening should be on demand. However, for all practical purposes, notice is required, as the A17 trunk road carries thousands of vehicles a day. A far cry from the late 19th century.

The bridge-keepers are invariably helpful as long as they are aware of your intentions. Having booked a bridge swing, maintain contact on approach on VHF 09, call sign 'Swing Bridge.' Reporting points should be on leaving the anchorage, at the lighthouses and on having the Port Sutton Bridge commercial quay in sight, where you should report your vessel as being at DOUBLE REDS. Proceed as

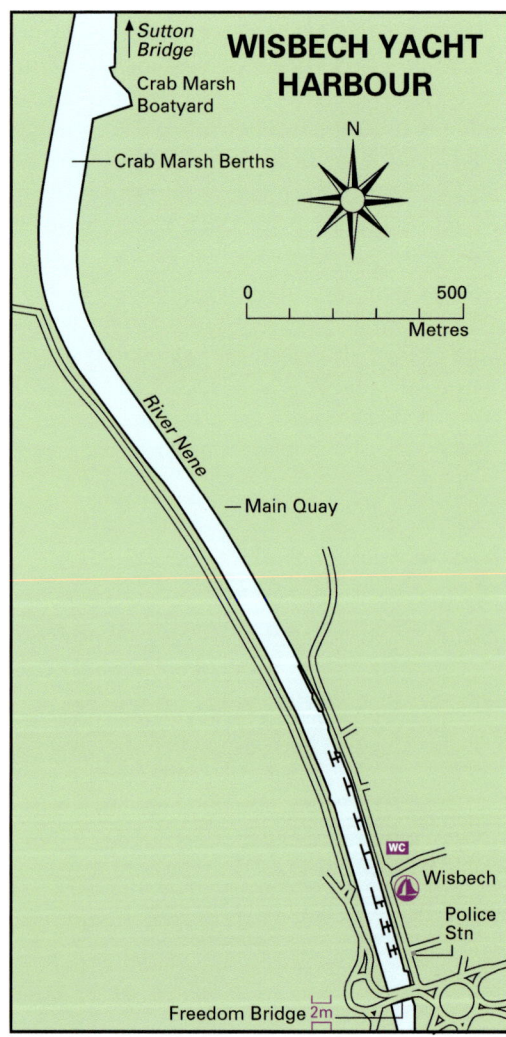

Wisbech

instructed by the bridge-keeper and obey the traffic signals on the bridge turret, committing only when GREEN lights are in your favour.

On spring tides there is every chance of sharing a bridge swing with a commercial ship bound to or from Wisbech. Needless to say the ship will have priority but the bridge-keeper will keep you appraised. Having cleared the bridge, the passage is between the banks with little variation for the next 6M. Both banks are well marked with lit beacons. Green to the west, red to east.

If your passage is delayed, or circumstances dictate a change of plan, updating the bridge-keeper is not only a courtesy but avoids unnecessary arrangements on his part.

As Wisbech is reached, the grassy banks recede and to the east, on the port hand, Crab Marsh Boatyard is evident with its ranks of craft laid up ashore and the 75T boat hoist. From here on, the east bank is made up of built quayside where much imported timber is stored. Commercial ships may well be berthed alongside.

It will not be long before the small craft pontoon moorings come into view which are all on the port hand, east bank.

Moorings

Make prior arrangements with Wisbech Yacht Harbour as to berth availability. This will result in a berth allocation, allowing a mental picture of where you are to come alongside – an important preparatory step here. Draught is a consideration to discuss too, but up to 2.5m can remain afloat even on LWS.

The natural tendency when heading for Wisbech is to arrive as soon as possible on a given tide. This is not necessarily a problem but, especially on springs, the risk is too much flood tide carrying you along faster than you would like.

Adopt the practice of commercial ships, and turn in the tideway well before your allocated berth. The ships do this in the swinging basin but small craft have room between the river banks, so one's 'swing' can be left later *but must be conducted before reaching the first of the pontoons*. Better early than late, and when the swing is completed, motoring ahead gives all the control necessary. Stem the tide and remain stationary over the ground while you gather your thoughts for coming alongside.

Easing back on the throttle will allow the vessel to gather sternway. Or, given a need to straighten up, a burst ahead does the trick. When level with the chosen berth or even upstream of it, easing alongside conventionally, or better still ferry gliding, completes the job without drama. There are no prizes for speed records. Welcome to Wisbech. You are in good company. Mariners have been doing this since Roman times.

Facilities and visitor information

All the moorings in Wisbech are serviced with water and electricity and the gates for access ashore are at both north and south ends. The gate code can be obtained from the harbour office in The Boathouse, the modern building on the quay which also houses toilets, showers, and laundry, and is a source of cards for shore power. Opt for the north gate unless going into the town when south is better.

As with Sutton Bridge, everything necessary is within walking distance, although on a larger scale, Wisbech having a population of over 30,000.

Needless to say, provisioning is simple with at least two major supermarkets within easy walking distance of the yacht harbour. Traditional markets are on Thursdays and Saturdays. Diesel is at the fuel berth and petrol and bottled gas from the BP petrol station within sight.

Wisbech Yacht Harbour, looking upstream towards Freedom Bridge

The Boathouse building above Wisbech Yacht Harbour
Fenland District Council

It is a thriving market town and in centuries past was one of England's principal ports. Agriculture and related industry is, in the main, what makes it tick. The majority of the country's fresh produce is grown in the vicinity and food processing provides much local employment.

The draining of the fens and the riverside location brought prosperity and from the late 18th and early 19th centuries, the port flourished. Its greatest ship owner was Richard Young, who at one time had some 43 trading vessels and, in 1853, even entered the age of steam with his 700 ton *Lady Alice Lambton*. At the time, she was the biggest vessel ever to have arrived here.

In the town on North and South Brinks, there is ample architectural evidence of this age of prosperity and Wisbech's Georgian buildings are enviable. Prime among these is Peckover House, built in 1722 and purchased by the Quaker Peckover banking family in the 1790s. Now owned by the National Trust, it was renamed in honour of the Peckovers whose Peckover Bank became part of Barclays. On the National Trust topic, one of that body's founders, the social reformer Octavia Hill, was born in Wisbech and a museum charting her life and achievements is on South Brink.

Another famous son of Wisbech was the abolitionist Thomas Clarkson who, with William Wilberforce, campaigned to bring about the end of the slave trade. A memorial to Clarkson stands near Town Bridge.

For those with an historical bent, a visit to the town's museum has much to commend it, not least the early photographic libraries of Samuel Smith and Lilian Ream which, as a social history, rival the works of Whitby's Frank Meadow Sutcliffe.

For those with more urgent tastes, the town's brewery, Elgood's, founded in 1795 and still in family hands, is open to the public and supplies many local hostelries.

While passenger railways are long gone from Wisbech, the bus station is very close and a fast, regular service to the cathedral cities of Peterborough to the west and Norwich to the east opens up the region and makes a longer stay in the safe haven of Wisbech worthy of consideration. The nice people in the tourist information office by the Clarkson Memorial will happily assist such planning.

Departure

A passage seawards requires early notification to the harbour office, if only to ascertain whether there are any commercial ship movements over your chosen departure tide. Passing ships under way in the river is to be avoided if at all possible. Similarly, early advice to Cross Keys Swing Bridge ensures a swing when it's wanted.

Concerning optimum time for leaving, a lesson can again be taken from commercial ships which take the ground on their berths but as they most often leave in ballast, that is without cargo, depart as soon as they float on the incoming tide. Small craft will not be aground, of course, but due to shallow points in the river, relevant until the flood begins, a preferred departure time would be predicted HW minus 2 hours 30. This, by the time you arrive at the river mouth, will enable carrying most of the ebb away. Having the benefit of as much of the ebb as possible until you are clear of The Wash is the ideal. But this does mean punching tide down to Sutton Bridge at least.

An alternative is a later departure, even at or around HW, then laying over at Sutton Bridge until the next tide. This allows you to depart Sutton Bridge on the last of the flood and enjoy the full ebb away with less need to push strong, incoming tide. Draught, best possible speed, and the point in the tidal cycle, will all serve to inform choice, but the harbour office will be happy to assist with any plan.

It would be improper not to make mention of the prospects for cruising upstream from Wisbech and the delights of the non-tidal river and indeed, beyond. For the right craft, a passage to Northampton is possible and from there, the Grand Union Canal. Or Fenland waterways via the Middle Level and thence the Great Ouse to Ely and Cambridge. These delights, though, are beyond the scope of this publication and are the subject of other titles from the publishers. However, introducing mariners to the less well known links between the tidal and non-tidal waterways in the region is appropriate as navigation on more and more regional waterways is improved. For example, at the time of writing, the Fens Waterways Link, joining Lincoln, Peterborough, Ely and Boston is well in hand and hailed as the biggest waterways improvement project in Europe.

Fosdyke and Boston

Fosdyke on the River Welland and Boston on the River Witham are Lincolnshire's principal havens on The Wash. Fosdyke no longer handles ships but its privately developed marina and boatyard have breathed new life into what otherwise would have been a bygone corner of the world. Boston remains a busy commercial port and the enclosed dock and river berths are typical coasting and short sea destinations.

Fosdyke is a very modest settlement and apart from the very welcoming Ship Inn, the boatyard would likely be the only objective for the visiting leisure sailor. The River Welland, some 65 miles in length and rising in Northamptonshire, runs through Stamford and Spalding and thence to its outfall, but for all practical purposes, it is not a boating prospect upstream of Fosdyke except for canoeists and paddleboarders.

Largely serving a vast, agricultural hinterland, Boston is a busy market town. For the leisure boater it also offers a link with an inland waterways system which, at the very least, allows those with suitable air draught to navigate to the cathedral city of Lincoln some 30 miles distant.

It should be noted, however, that at the time of writing, there are no all-tide small craft moorings for visitors on the River Witham below the Grand Sluice sea lock. You should not enter the Witham speculatively. The Grand Sluice lock maximum vessel dimensions are, subject to variation of river level, LOA 20.2m x Beam 5.3m x draught 1.52m x Air draught 2.74m.

Boston nonetheless offers much from any perspective and moves are afoot to provide suitable moorings for the visitor from seaward.

Approaches to the Rivers Welland and Witham

Up to the Tabs Head pillar beacon, a sector light Q WG 4m 1M, the approach is common to both rivers. The beacon is in position 52°56'·00N 000°4'·92E, immediately off both river mouths, and carries a tide gauge.

To this point, approach from seaward is likely via the North Well SWM and Roaring Middle SWM then a course of 256° for 3.75M to the start of the Freeman Channel. This is the deep-water route into Lower Road, the extension of Boston Deep.

Norfolk, The Wash and Humber

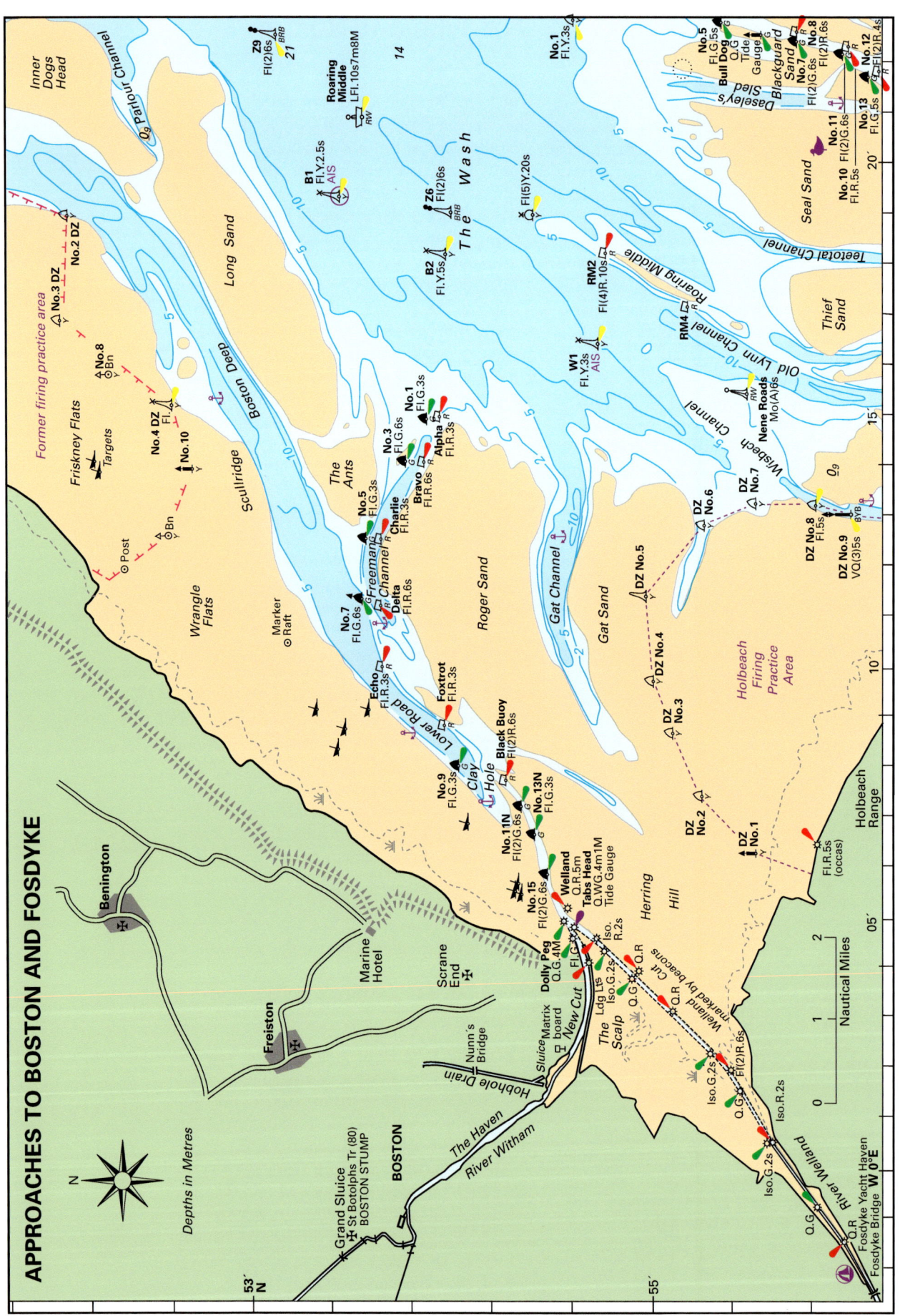

Be aware that as the Freeman merges into Lower Road, between The Ants and Roger Sand, there is a shallower ridge in the vicinity of Delta PHM with a least charted depth of 2.2m. However, as with all the rivers of The Wash, a final approach before local HW -3hrs is not recommended, after which time this feature will not constrain the usual cruising yacht. If earlier on the tide, anchoring out of the channel, near to the Delta PHM is an option.

An inshore approach which might suit those coasting from the north is between Inner Knock sand and Outer Dogs Head in the northwest corner of The Wash, off Gibraltar Point. This route leads into Boston Deep and then Lower Road. Sadly, this channel is no longer buoyed but it does exist, as evidenced by a survey in 2020 and reflected in the subsequent chart revisions. With care, especially around LW when sands can be clearly seen, and given favourable weather, this route is an attractive option. It also makes Wainfleet Haven readily available for the shoal draught cruiser.

The Wainfleet former firing practice area remains marked by unlit, yellow DZ special marks which provide a useful visual reference. These buoys are still on station to warn against straying over the range where unexploded ordnance may lay unrecovered.

For the unhurried visitor, anchoring inside Long Sand off Scullridge is a far from crowded place to pause, even overnight. Unless you are averse to the company of seals, it can be idyllic.

Landward features are few save for St. Botolph's Church tower, The Boston Stump, which is conspicuous in good visibility. At 83m it is one of the tallest Medieval church towers in the country.

Fosdyke

It's difficult not to like what's been achieved at Fosdyke since the commercial wharf ceased trading. A wholly private, entrepreneurial venture, Fosdyke Yacht Haven (FYH) has broken new ground and impressed itself firmly on the east coast boating scene. Catering for owners both local and from throughout the East Midlands, the range of services is impressive and now includes boat building. Something long since missing from all the ports on The Wash.

Useful information – River Welland for Fosdyke

Fairway buoy Freeman Channel No.1 SHM Fl.G. 3s. 52°57′·83N 00°15′·00E

Buoyed channel As charted. Rivers confluence at Tabs Head sector light. Q.WG.

Moorings River Welland. Fosdyke Yacht Haven.
☎ +44 1205260240/ +44 77768 817272

Contacts
Harbour Authority Fosdyke Yacht Haven ☎ +44 1205 260240
www.fosdykeyachthaven.co.uk

VHF Port Working Channel No VHF for River Welland.

Tidal predictions based on Tabs Head tide gauge.

Charts Admiralty 1200 and Imray Y9

Ever mindful of the needs of the yachting fraternity, the founder, David Parkinson, even bought and refurbished the local inn. The Ship has built a wider than local reputation for its fare and is a good reason to visit.

Approaches

Tabs Head is the confluence of the two rivers and from here it's just under 6M to the bridge in Fosdyke. On leaving Tabs Head to starboard, Welland Cut is the initial stretch for 3.5M through the inter-tidal area. The channel is bound by training walls and marked with beacons, some lit, and stakes. The course throughout is virtually straight and starts at least on 222°.

As the land rises, the river banks become more distinct and the waterway narrower. At the pylons, (23m), there is less than 1M to run and time to prepare to come alongside.

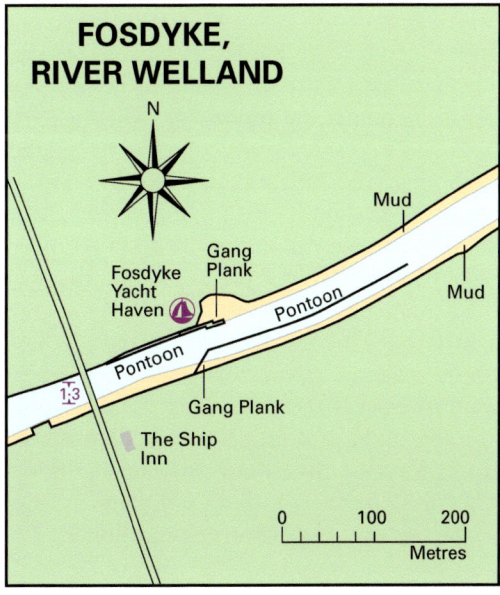

Norfolk, The Wash and Humber

Fosdyke Yacht Haven looking seaward

Tabs Head sector light serving both Witham and Welland

While there is always water in the river, it is best to plan arrival close to local HW, not only to ensure sufficient depth in the lower reach but to avoid an uncomfortable rate of tidal set at passage end. On springs, 5 kts or more is not unusual and Fosdyke Bridge, carrying the A17 trunk road, has an air draught of only 1.3m at MHWS.

Prudence dictates an advance arrangement with the marina to agree a designated berth. The local practice is to swing in the tideway before reaching the moorings, which are to both sides of the river. Once swung and stemming the tide, under control, it is relatively straightforward to allow the tide to set you astern, or to nudge ahead as required once you are off your designated berth, turn the helm gently and ferry glide alongside. Be aware that closer to the bridge there is less room to swing.

Of course, if the tide is just beginning to ebb, berthing is straightforward against the flow. Warping the boat round on the berth prior to departure, rather than manoeuvring in the tideway, is a risk-free evolution.

Moorings

Fosdyke pontoon berths are all afloat, fully serviced, secure and well patronised and though the essential business is around the permanent berths, Fosdyke is welcoming to visitors.

It has to be said that depths vary according to berth but even on LWS you are unlikely to find less than 1m, and more than 2m is possible.

Facilities and visitor information

50T boat lift, chandlery and a broad range of marine trades on site. The Moorings Café, a short walk away, is guaranteed to satisfy any breakfast taste and craving before sailing.

The River Welland was once a trading artery to Spalding and beyond but, for reasons various, its use as a navigable waterway has waned over time. It nevertheless remains tidal to just below Spalding and the non-tidal reaches are well used recreationally. Spalding even has a water taxi service in the town.

Boston

Tidal Barrier

This recent feature, 5M from the river mouth, is closed when there is a risk of tidal flooding or, on occasions, for maintenance. Warning of closure is promulgated by various means and at New Cut, immediately inward of the river mouth, a matrix message board is illuminated if the barrier is raised. In this instance you should return to sea or head to Fosdyke. Enquiry in advance can be made of the harbour authority (see 'Useful information').

Approaches

As with the other rivers of The Wash, entry at the mouth, unless in a shoal draught craft, will be HW -3hrs at the earliest and more probably nearer HW -2hrs. This could, particularly over springs, mean encountering commercial shipping and monitoring VHF 12 is important. Tabs Head is a reporting point. Call 'Boston Port Control' or if requiring clarification of intentions, call 'Boston Pilots' or even the ship concerned. A chat with the pilot himself could avoid embarrassment. Pilotage is compulsory for vessels over 30m LOA.

Useful information – River Witham for Boston

Fairway buoy Freeman Channel No. 1 SHM Fl.G. 3s. 52°57'·83N 000°15'·00E

Buoyed channel As charted. Rivers confluence at Tabs Head sector light. Q.WG.

Moorings River Witham. Only above sea lock. (Grand Sluice). Air draught restrictions apply. Lock Keeper ☏ +44 7387 050967. Boston Gateway Marina ☏ +44 1205 364420

Contacts
Environment Agency (EA) ☏ +44 205 364864 / +44 7712 010920
Harbour Authority Port of Boston. ☏ +44 1205 365571
www.victoriagroup/about-us/port-of-boston

VHF Port Working Channel VHF 12 River Witham.

Tidal predictions based on Tabs Head tide gauge.

Charts Admiralty 1200 and Imray Y9

Leaving Tabs Head to port and Dolly Peg SH Beacon Q G 4m 1M to starboard brings you into New Cut where the banks are not adjacent but the channel is marked with beacons to both port and starboard. After 2M, Hobshole Drain enters on the starboard hand and at Jolly Sailor 2 FG (vert), the river narrows and the channel becomes more defined. From here it's approximately 4M to the Grand Sluice.

Dolly Peg SH Beacon at River Witham mouth

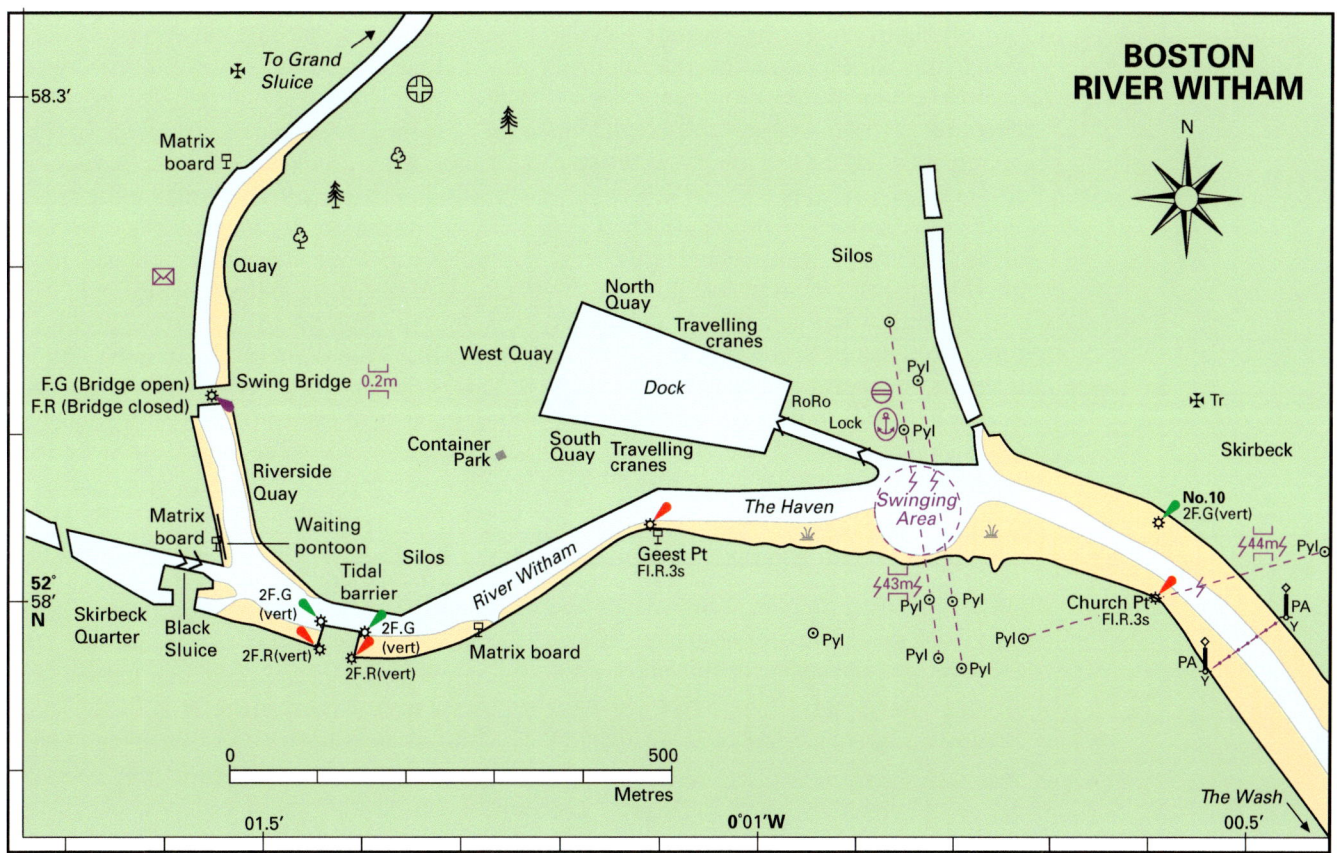

Norfolk, The Wash and Humber

River Witham at No.10 2 F.G (vert.) showing shoaling and beacons

After the pylons and overhead electricity cables (44m), the river bends westwards. The commercial dock entrance is via the ship lock at the swinging hole, where vessels up to 120m LOA can be found manoeuvring. Enlargement of the port's ship lock is the next marine civil project and temporary restrictions might apply in this vicinity until further notice.

Less than 0.5M on from here is the tidal barrier which is now operational. The tidal barrier has resulted in reduced river width and the aperture (25m) is marked with fixed G and R lights. Note that vessels passing through the barrier with the tide in their favour have priority. Matrix message boards advise of barrier status and reporting requirements. At the barrier, International Port Traffic Signals apply.

Both above and below the barrier there are lengths of newly constructed quayside. Mooring chains are available for use by vessels in transit but constrained by barrier closure. Emergency landing is possible via ladders. It is not to be assumed that vessels securing here will remain afloat over a LW and these moorings should be used only when transit through the barrier is not possible.

Moorings in Boston and on the Witham

Boston. So much to offer, but where's the essential link to life ashore? In a nutshell, it isn't there – yet. So, the advice of this pilot, as of now, is not to enter the River Witham without having a mooring arrangement in place.

As with all The Wash rivers, siltation is a perennial problem but in Boston, once the tide is away, the levels of accretion are considerable. As such, at low water, while the river banks are clearly defined by built quayside, virtually all moored craft take the ground, some at less than desirable angles. All this is a great pity given the potential of Boston's waterfront.

Boston is also home to a number of inshore commercial fishing boats which use quayside moorings so the small craft scene, such as it is, is a mixed one. Shoreside access is inevitably by vertical ladder and the bottom is not guaranteed fair. All in all, mooring at random and hoping for the best is not recommended.

Contrast this picture with the £100 million plus Boston Barrier which is now complete. This barrier, just above the commercial port and principally a flood defence measure, was also intended to provide water level management, impounding water through Boston Haven with access for small craft via a sea lock in the barrier structure. This for the economic and environmental benefit and to enhance navigation. Sadly, this element of the scheme fell by the wayside for want of the installation of a small lock or even a flap gate during the barrier construction.

One can but hope it is not off the agenda into perpetuity, although how much easier it would have been to incorporate before the civil contractors demobilised. The net result of someone's red pencil, however, is that Boston is not, for the meantime, part of the vastly improved 'offer' to small craft sailors in the immediate region, and the envisaged stable water level, encouraging boats to moor and visit the town, will not be realised.

Once through the barrier, on the port hand is the Black Sluice lock and pumping station. This is the entrance to the South Forty Foot Drain, an artificial waterway now re-opened to navigation for some 19M west of Boston, although there are presently no permanent moorings available. Part of the Fens Waterways Link, much is promised in due course by way of inland passage making.

Enquiries over access through the Black Sluice Lock should be made to the Environment Agency (EA) lock keeper. (See 'Useful information', page 51.)

Immediately upstream of the Black Sluice and on the same hand is a pontoon mooring for vessels waiting for the lock. Without doubt this is a tempting prospect for visitors. However, there is no ready shoreside access, no guarantee of sufficient depth at LW, nor can the bottom be considered fair if taking the ground. This is a sorry waste of a facility for want of some adaption and management but could, of course, be utilised with care.

It is worth noting that the Black Sluice, as with other drainage channels does, from time to time release flood water into the tidal river. This can result in rates of flow in excess of the norm, if only at the point of discharge.

The next feature upstream is the railway swing bridge. This is usually open to river traffic. Boston Port Control can advise as to status. The deepest water is to the west bank.

From here to the Haven Bridge there are moorings to both banks, some quayside, some to staging, but none are public. The previous caveats over their suitability remain.

Above Haven Bridge is Town Bridge, a cast iron structure dating from 1913. This is the lowest bridge encountered in the tideway. Here is the critical air draught factor when inward on a rising tide. The bridge soffit at point of maximum clearance is 9.2m above the level of the Boston dock sill and the tidal predictions in the local tide tables, available on the Port of Boston website are relative to dock sill. Variations on prediction can occur however given conditions of wind and weather but Boston Port Control can advise as to tide height in real time.

Immediately above the Town Bridge is St. Botolph's Footbridge. From here the Grand Sluice and its lock to the east bank can be clearly seen.

For unmasted vessels, there is a congenial prospect above The Grand Sluice sea lock. Above the lock, all afloat moorings await, plus the facilities at both Boston Gateway Marina and Witham Sailing Club. Thereafter, 35M of navigation to the cathedral city of Lincoln.

Lock dimensions are the restricting factor, particularly air draught. The controlling authority, The Canal and River Trust, quote 2.74m as a maximum but this is a guide and can vary according to river level. For example, the author knows of at least one local boat with an air draught of 3.3m which regularly transits the lock. First point of contact then is with the lock keeper to discuss intentions. ☏ +44 7387 050967.

Boston, being a town of over 35,000 population, has all the usual facilities in terms of provisioning and recreation. For reasons which will have become apparent though, if not enjoying a non-tidal mooring with Boston Gateway Marina, showers and toilets are lacking, so unless the visitor has been fortunate enough to identify a suitable overnight berth and is self-sufficient by way of sanitation, a rustic visit could ensue.

Doubly sad then that as part of the Black Sluice development, a café with showers and toilets was included adjacent to the canal basin. This currently has to rely on local rather than waterborne trade.

And while the commercial fishing fleet does require maintenance and repair, it is usual now for them to take advantage of Fosdyke for the purpose, so marine trades and chandlery are no longer available here.

Top: Railway Swing Bridge, Boston from upstream showing typical local moorings

Bottom: Grand Sluice sea lock from the non-tidal side showing air draught restriction

Wainfleet Haven

At the northwest extreme of The Wash lies Gibraltar Point, familiar to all who cock more than half an ear to the BBC shipping forecast, in particular the inshore predictions when 'Whitby to Gibraltar Point' and 'Gibraltar Point to North Foreland' get the attention.

Tucked behind the headland is the outfall of the River Steeping upon which lies Wainfleet Haven, an ancient port serving Wainfleet All Saints, an historically significant market town.

Wainfleet is home to the Gibraltar Point Sailing Club, (GPSC), another of those creek-based, DIY bands of enthusiasts who are the difference between such locations being managed for the common good or silting up and disappearing. Long may they prosper.

While including Wainfleet in a cruising itinerary is for the shoal draughted, and possibly looked back upon as a rustic experience, nothing should be discounted. Between Inner Dogs Head and Outer Dogs Head in position 53°3'·81N 000°22'·38E lies a LW anchorage amongst the sands around a 5m contour. Open to the east but otherwise sheltered. An alternative is inside Outer Dogs Head in position 53°4'·57N 000°20'·79E.

The club welcome is inevitably warm and there is much to enjoy in the vicinity, especially if a bike or two are aboard.

Useful information – Wainfleet

Fairway buoy SHM WH Fl G 5s in position 53°04'·79N 000°20'·17E

Buoyed channel 1M+ across inter-tidal flats. Marks are varied type and some are lit.

Moorings Up river on the starboard hand after turn to port. Staging with ladders. All moorings dry to soft mud bottom.

Contacts GPSC Commodore
☏ +44 7754 950564
Harbour Authority Within Port of Boston jurisdiction but local contact is the Gibraltar Point Sailing Club www.gpsc.org.uk

VHF Port Working Channel No dedicated channel.

Tidal predictions based on Skegness.

Hazards Entry possible only over HW and according to draught and height of tide. Buoyed channel can vary. Decommissioned MoD bombing range nearby but unexploded ordnance can remain. Yellow special marks denote boundary.

Charts Admiralty 108 Imray Y9

GPSC moorings at Wainfleet at high tide *Andy Dingle*

Wainfleet Haven

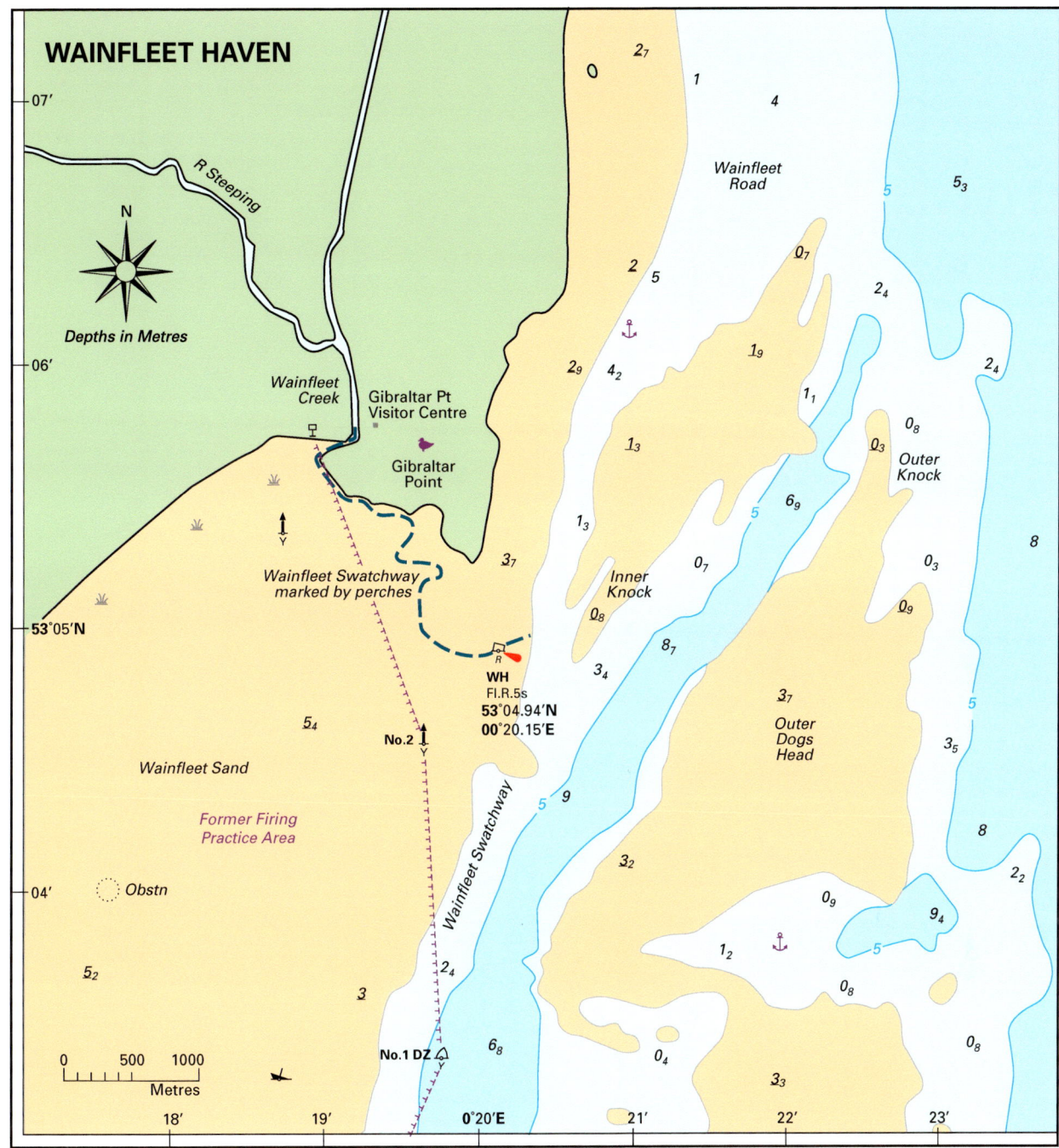

Approaches

The sadness is that while this area is within the jurisdiction of the Port of Boston Authority, buoyage here is a thing of the past for want of commercial justification. Nevertheless, a deep-water channel remains between Inner Knock and Outer Dogs Head as confirmed by a survey of 2020 in support of the Sail The Wash marine tourism project. From position 53°7'·88N 000°24'·44E when the Lynn Wind Farm southwest corner Y Special Mark Fl.Y 5s 5M bears 111°, steer a COG of 215° then via 53°6'·35N 000°22'·78E and 53°4'·58N 000°20'·80E. Here is Wainfleet Swatchway where the locally placed, unlit beacons and perches mark the channel over Wainfleet Sand to the River Steeping entrance.

From further into The Wash and The Well, Parlour Channel was once an option into Boston Deep when it was buoyed but again, this is no longer so and The Parlour awaits an up-to-date survey (see plan page 48). Until then, unless with good local knowledge or a willingness to sound one's own way in calm weather, Parlour Channel is not recommended.

Norfolk, The Wash and Humber

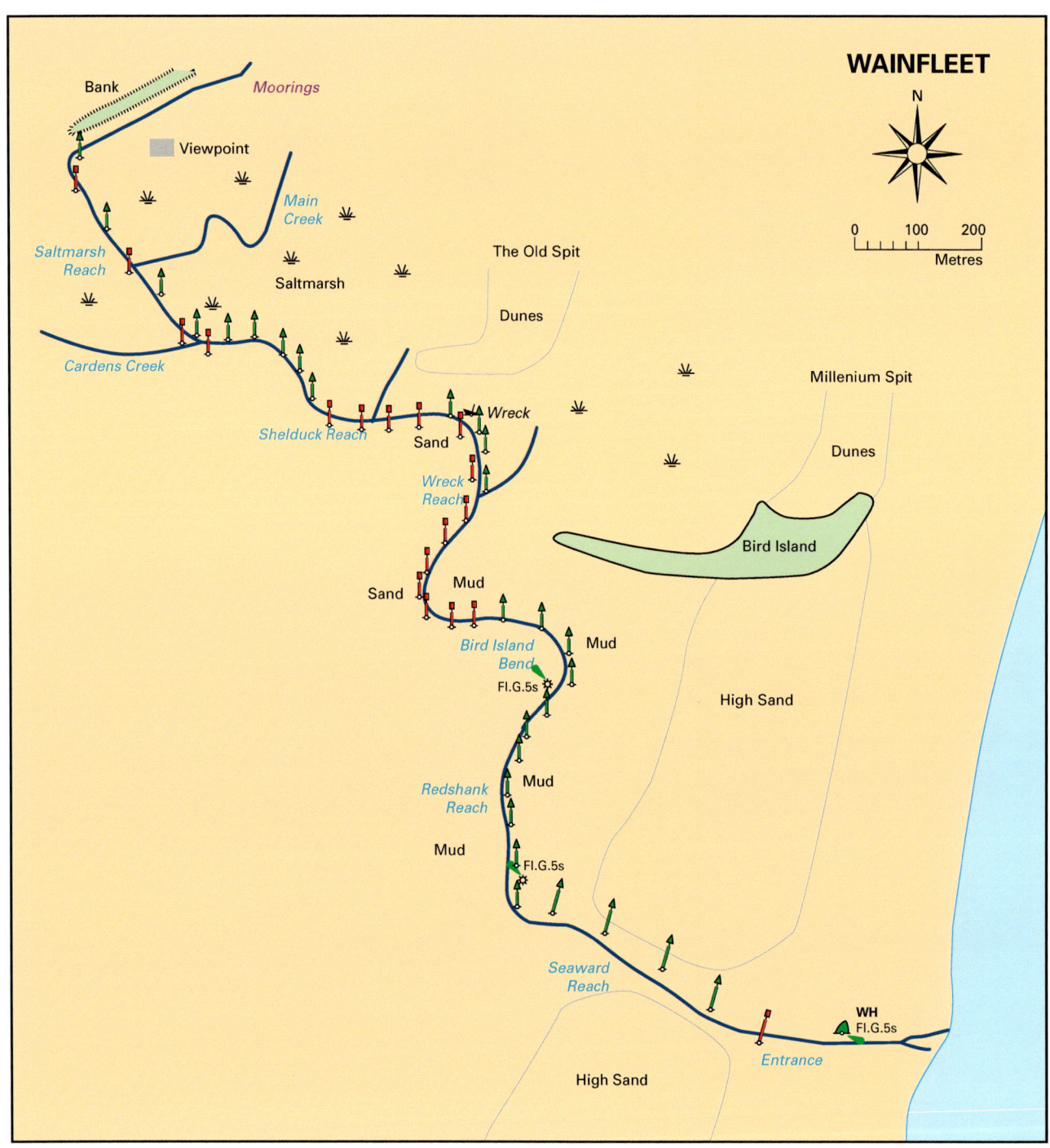

Information provided by Ian Martin of Gibraltar Point Sailing Club

Entry

The course of Wainfleet Swatchway changes frequently and it's the good people of GPSC who ensure perches, pellet buoys, spar buoys and beacons (which are numerous and conspicuous), follow suit. They also transfer these changes to a chartlet, available via their website www.gpsc.org.uk. A call ahead too is sensible if intending to visit, which at the very least will ensure an entry passage benefits from the latest local knowledge. Contact GPSC Commodore – contact details on the website.

This haven is suitable only for shoal draughted craft and as a general guide, if drawing 1.5m, local HW – 2hrs would be a good minimum or HW – 1hr if on neaps. Tidal predictions for Skegness are relevant.

The fairway buoy equivalent is a SHM WH Fl.G 5s in position 53°04'·79N 00°20'·17E. Thereafter there is just over 1M of winding channel across the inter-tidal flats.

Once inside the sea bank, the course of the river is clearer despite small tributaries which could deceive. The river winds but bankside beacons assist and the banks themselves are defined even on a big tide.

Moorings

All moorings are on the starboard hand as you head inward and the first encountered are those of the few local inshore fishing boats which call Wainfleet their home port. Thereafter the river bends to port and the GPSC moorings, all wooden staging, come into view. There are no public or dedicated visitor moorings. Pot luck is the order of the day, which is why a call ahead to the Commodore is advisable.

Beware the run of tide as room for manoeuvre is limited and beyond the extent of the moorings is a foot bridge and sluice which is the effective extent of navigation. At the inward extreme is the club slipway where, by using the creek opposite and backing and filling, a 180° turn can be effected before motoring back downstream and mooring port side to. Local custom and practice though, is to nudge the bow into the accommodating west bank and let the tide do the work.

All moorings dry out, of course, but soft mud and an absence of a foul bottom is generally the case.

Facilities and visitor information

The GPSC clubhouse is the first recourse after a testing passage, but assuming members will be in residence might disappoint. Weekends, as with many like clubs are hives of activity, however, and any yacht taking the trouble to nose into the Wainfleet will be welcomed as long as there's someone there to do it.

There is one very good reason to visit Wainfleet, that being the Gibraltar Point Nature Reserve and Visitor Centre which is close by. Administered by the Lincolnshire Wildlife Trust, this reserve runs as far as Skegness and is that dynamic stretch of coastline habitat for terns, skylarks, flocks of waders and much else. The modern visitor centre includes café and toilets and, while not aimed at the passing leisure sailor, it can represent a haven in its own right.
www.lincstrust.org.uk/get-involved/top-reserves/gibraltar-point

For a wider range of attractions, expeditionary talents will have to be employed. For provisions and links with wider civilisation, a 3 mile venture is required. Two options: Skegness, for the traditional seaside experience, is northwards up a good, sealed road, ideal for those with bicycles aboard. Skegness railway station makes for connection further afield and the Poacher Line, a community rail service, has hourly services to Nottingham and points in between.
www.poacherline.org.uk

One such halt is at Wainfleet All Saints. This market town on the River Steeping once enjoyed a robust coastal shipping trade with Hull and was, at one time, on the coast itself. Batemans Brewery is a local feature whose fare is readily available from the usual sources and brewery tours have merit. A supermarket and a range of independent shops cater for most tastes and the museum and library are worthwhile diversions.

Between these points is Havenhouse Station, the nearest public transport link with Wainfleet moorings. Taxis ply from both Skegness and Wainfleet All Saints.

Wainfleet staging when the tide recedes

Norfolk, The Wash and Humber

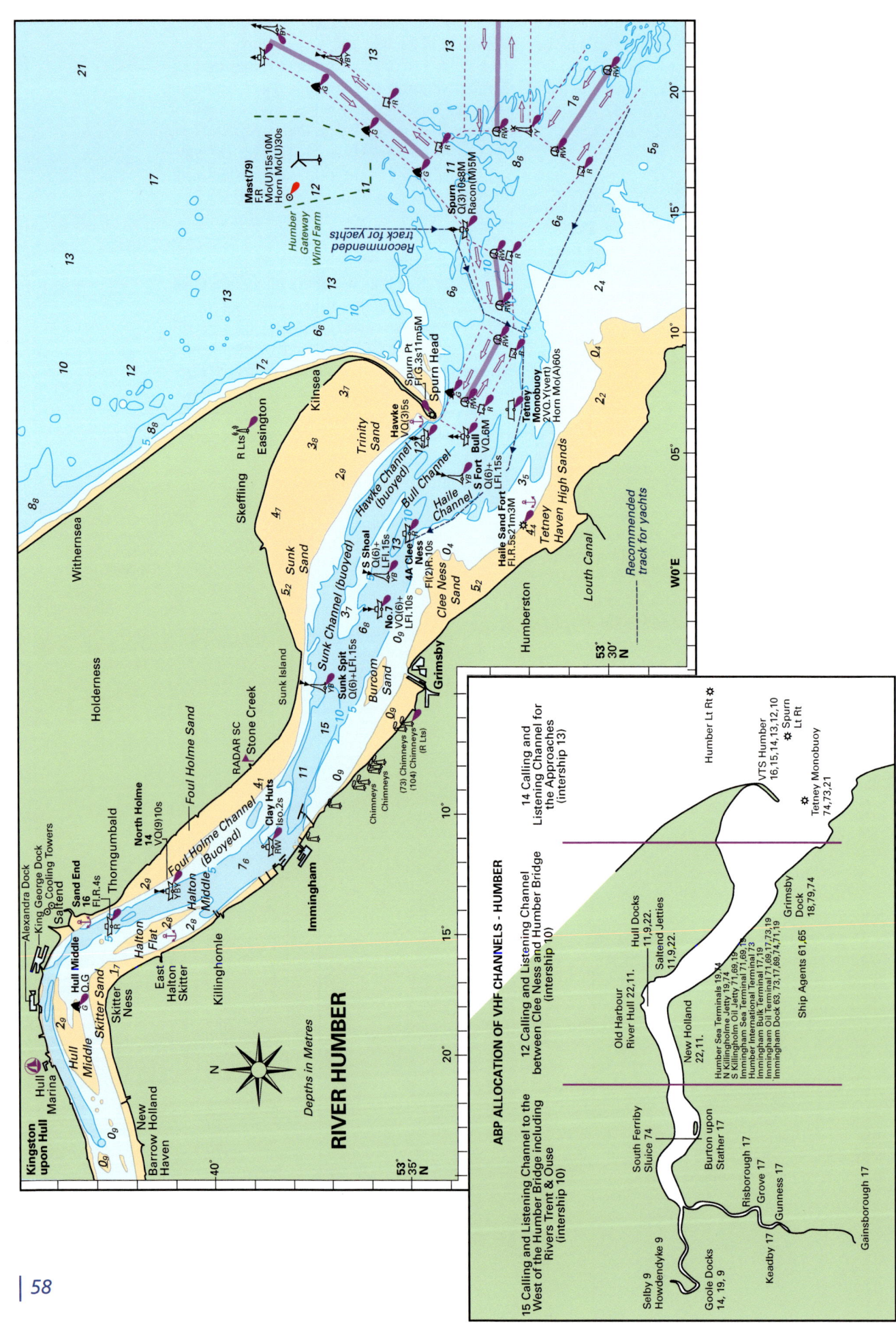

THE HUMBER

'A long, testing beat from the south, hard on the wind was nearing an end as dusk crept across the Spurn. The calm of the dock in Grimsby was within reach; just 10 miles to run and thoughts turned to what the corkscrew's for. The wind remained fresh but at last we could bear away. And as we did, we took off like the proverbial rocket.'

Styled routinely as the River Humber, this vast expanse of tidal water, 4M wide at its mouth, is strictly speaking not a river but an estuary, fed by the Rivers Ouse and Trent and to a lesser extent the Rivers Ancholme, Hull and Freshney further downstream.

Presenting to the eye as if you could sail anywhere, being over 1M wide at the Humber Bridge and 4M wide at the mouth, the Humber can and does accommodate some of the largest deep-sea vessels and is ranked third amongst UK rivers by most commercial measures. Even a cursory study of the relevant charts however, suggests a different story and it's worth remembering that on at least two occasions in recent times, this waterway has been crossed on foot upstream of the Humber Bridge. Swimming across it is not unusual either.

The Humber's claims to fame are various. Noted in Roman records it is also acknowledged in Ptolemy's *Geographia*. Historically it formed a boundary between Anglo-Saxon kingdoms. Strategic in times of war, the forts from the First World War still stand in the mouth and remain valuable as visual references.

Built in 1981, the Humber Bridge was, at the time, the world's longest single span suspension bridge. Prior to its opening, ferries had plied the waterway for centuries and the service between Hessle and Barton-upon-Humber, where the bridge starts and finishes, was mentioned in the Domesday Book.

Hull and Grimsby were once centres of Britain's fishing industry. While much fish is still processed in Grimsby, none is now landed there. The picture in Hull is similar and although Brexit was, for some, to be the salvation of British fishing interests, it is only the industry heritage centres that are left to tell the story.

Ecologically the Humber remains vitally important. In 2019, following a sixty-year absence, river oysters were re-introduced. Many fish species migrate here, heading to spawning grounds upstream. Over-wintering birds abound. Even bitterns can be spotted or heard. The Severn-Trent flyway, the cross-country corridor used by migratory birds, starts and finishes here.

Fifty miles inland lies the port of Goole, gateway to much of the country's canal network. For those with the right boat, navigation to the city of York is a prospect not to be dismissed lightly.

All in all, though marina access needs thought, committing a few days to the Humber from a longer cruise is unlikely to disappoint. It is more than just a haven from adverse weather when transiting the east coast, though its tactical anchorages are worth noting as places of refuge.

Given the constraints of most of the drying havens surrounding the Humber, it would be easy to find reasons to pass them by but this would be a mistake as there are more ways than one of enjoying what they offer.

As this pilot describes elsewhere, conventional, all afloat facilities exist on both banks of the estuary and a preparedness to leave the boat and be a land borne tourist for a day can bring its rewards. Public transport serves the area well and links the smaller havens touched upon in this publication. An evening at the chart table poring over a few timetables can pay dividends to those of an enquiring disposition.

It is not the place of this pilot to be proscriptive over how anyone organises time spent on the Humber but it will not escape any readers' notice that the smaller, tidal havens have limited mooring facility, at least in contemporary terms. That any or all might be discounted as places to take a boat would, at one level, not be a surprise. It is hoped nonetheless that the descriptions of the respective towns and villages will whet an appetite or two and spawn an enthusiasm to visit, one way or another.

Charts

Of particular importance is having up to date charts including the Humber west of the Humber Bridge. Associated British Ports Humber is the harbour authority and because of the extensive and ever-changing shoaling in the estuary, a regular programme of hydrographic surveying is undertaken by them.

This results in a series of local ABP charts, some updated at least every two months and covering the entire estuary, including the port limits seaward of the mouth, then inland up to Keadby on the River Trent and Skelton Bridge on the River Ouse. You would be unwise to navigate the Humber, especially upstream of the Humber Bridge, without a recent copy of an ABP chart. These are readily available from two local chart agents or can be viewed at no charge on the ABP website (see 'Useful information', page 63).

Tides

One further factor which will impinge on passage planning within the estuary and its rivers concerns tides. At Spurn Head, at the Humber mouth, the duration of ebb and flood tides will be approximately equal. Further upstream and as a result of shallower water and fluvial flow, this is not the case.

For example, approaching Apex Light (Trent Falls), a flood tide duration can be of 4hrs and the ebb 8.5hrs. Higher up the Trent in Gainsborough, the difference can be considerably greater with a spring flood of just 2.5hrs and the ebb running for 10hrs.

Apart from the bearing this has on passage timing, it means too that a flood tide, once it begins can see a rise in height of as much as 1m in 10 minutes. Something over which those in charge of small vessels need to take account.

Around the Humber and its rivers there are sixteen electronic tide gauges transmitting data to VTS Humber continuously. Readings are in relation to charted depths at each location. There are also many visual tide gauge boards which are similarly calibrated. These represent a ready source of real-time tidal height information for mariners to confirm available water and VTS Humber, via the relevant VHF channel will relay this on request.

Shipping

Approximately 40,000 commercial shipping movements occur here annually and such vessels are invariably constrained by their draught. Their speed over the ground can also be three times that of small craft. Separation zones are in force through the outer approaches and Vessel Traffic Services (VTS) monitor by VHF and radar. Rules 9 and 18 of the International Regulations for Preventing Collisions at Sea should be strictly adhered to.

Commercial vessels of any size could be bound for or leaving various docks and terminals on either bank, shaping courses other than upstream or down and therefore found on converging courses at any time. Tidal set can mean a ship's head does not reflect her course over the ground.

In general, sufficient water exists for small craft outside the main, buoyed channels at most states of the tide.

Port VHF channels vary according to zone, of which there are three. (See diagram, page 58.) Small craft should monitor the appropriate channel and not hesitate to communicate with Humber VTS if in need of clarification. There is merit in reporting your vessel's name, position, intentions, and souls on board as a matter of routine.

There are broadcasts of weather and navigational warnings at 3 minutes past each hour.

Anchorages

Immediately inside the Humber mouth there are some possible anchorages. On the south shore of the Humber, Tetney Haven is the first anchoring location inside the mouth providing shelter from winds from the southwest.

If the weather is from the north or east, shelter inside Spurn bight can be found and a yellow mooring buoy is there for exactly that purpose. From Hawke EC Light Float VQ (3) 5s, run in towards the high and low disused lighthouses and the jetty, off which will likely be the RLNI lifeboat. The yacht mooring buoy is just northward of the lifeboat. The RNLI station here is the only one permanently manned and by fully employed crew. Visitors should feel free to donate.

If anchoring, there is deep water in this vicinity but be mindful depths change in the estuary. Further in towards the disused lighthouses, it dries. The holding is good. Sand and shell. For those with the means of going ashore, The Crown and Anchor PH in Kilnsea is but a short, bracing walk away.

Upstream of Spurn Point on the north shore, another location offers scope for anchoring. To the north of S9 SHM in the Sunk Dredged Channel lies Hawkins Point which can provide some shelter from the northwest.

> **Donna Nook Firing Range** has been in continual use since the First World War when it was established to protect targets on the Humber from enemy airship incursion. It is now a national nature reserve, the only one in the UK on Ministry of Defence land. It's also home to a large population of common and grey seals which, presumably, regard the activities of various air forces as great spectator sport.

TIDAL HAVENS OF THE HUMBER

Saltfleet

On the south shore of the Humber on the somewhat featureless Lincolnshire coast close to Mablethorpe, Saltfleet is one of those places where a group of friendly and enthusiastic leisure sailors, given the right weather, have a degree of fun out of all proportion to the facilities they have at their disposal. Specifically, the members of the Saltfleet Haven Boat Club. Long may it continue.

For the casual visitor however, irrespective of the warmth of welcome they would undoubtedly receive, entering without local knowledge would fly in the face of local advice. An extract from the club's website gives a flavour.

'We strongly recommend that every new member views the channel at low and high water before venturing out alone. We can arrange for someone to take you in the tractor at low water or by boat when the tide is in.'

Add to this the fact only one visitor mooring is available and if that is occupied then no room at the inn. Hence the need to look upon Saltfleet not as a refuge but as somewhere for a visit given planning and liaison with the boat club in advance.

Bear in mind that typical boat size here is no bigger than 25ft LOA and all are bilge or drop keel or small power boats which can sit comfortably on the soft mud.

Overall, be guided by the advice on the boat club website www.saltfleethaven.co.uk and speak with the Commodore on ☎ +44 7808 774868. Remember too that in NE winds, Saltfleet is a non-starter.

Local attractions include The New Inn and The Crown.

Tetney

On approaching the Humber the Lincolnshire coast appears featureless, but this belies what's beyond. As any crow will avow, it is not long, when flying inland, before the Lincolnshire Wolds reveal how spectacular is the countryside, well justifying its status as an Area of Outstanding Natural Beauty. Little more than 10 miles from Tetney lies Louth, a market town since the 8th century and known in these parts as the 'Capital of the Wolds,' with some justification. And just for the record, the immediate region spawned Alfred Lord Tennyson and Sir John Franklin, both educated in the local grammar school.

Before the coming of the railways, the prosperity of Louth was greatly enhanced by the construction of the Louth Canal, the canalisation of the River Lud, which discharges into the Humber. The canal has long since become un-navigable but neither Tetney Haven, at the seaward end of the tidal reach below the outfall sluice, nor the nearby village of Tetney have been idle following the canal's closing in 1924. Their more recent history includes an international telecommunications station from which the first radio link with Australia was established by the Marconi company in 1927. And during the 1960s and 70s at Tetney Lock, Bristow Helicopters ran a service delivering personnel to North Sea oil and gas rigs. Current industrial activity centres on the Tetney oil terminal which stores unrefined product discharged via the Tetney Monobuoy (52°32'·37N 000°6'·77E). This facility enables deep draughted tankers to offload in the roadstead rather than alongside. Cargoes are then pumped through a sub-sea pipeline to the oil refinery near Immingham, further up the Humber.

Of more immediate interest to the small craft visitor will be Tetney Haven itself and the facilities offered by the Humber Mouth Yacht Club (HMYC). This friendly and active club maintains moorings near the channel as well as the navigation marks which demand constant monitoring and when required, moving.

Approach and anchorage

Tetney Haven is the seaward extension of the Louth Canal and the resulting channel flows through the inter-tidal area towards Haile Sand Fort.

Good holding in sand and shell between the 5m and 2m contours. The Humber Mouth YC fairway buoy is adjacent. A drying bank here is known locally as The Whaleback. Anchoring off and in its lea provides additional shelter from weather from the west or southwest.

Anchoring anywhere in a fairway is prohibited, unless in an emergency.

Norfolk, The Wash and Humber

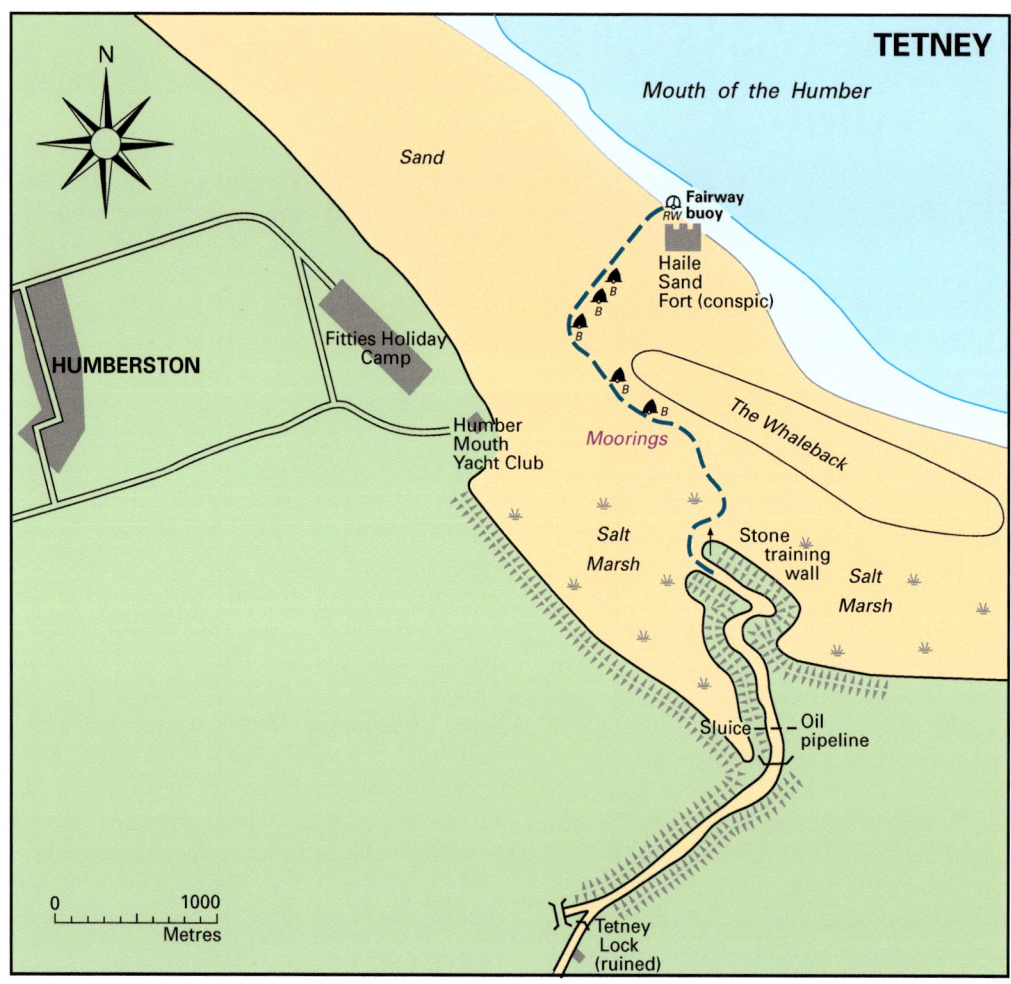

Entry to the channel is in the vicinity of Haile Sand Fort, 53°32'·09N 000°2'·02E FL.R 5s 21m 3M, where the HMYC maintained fairway buoy is also situated. This First World War fort, a circular concrete structure topped by a mast, is a conspicuous waymark. Depths vary in the vicinity of the fort, and immediately to landward it can dry on bigger tides.

Entry and moorings

Anyone venturing in without first having made contact with HMYC should be aware that anchoring in the channel itself is to be avoided. The banks are steep to and any boat drying out here could find itself at an uncomfortable angle. The swinging moorings are laid where they are for this reason even though there is water in the channel for longer.

Channel access is approximately HW +/- 2h. Club craft are typically up to 28ft LOA drawing 1.5m at most. The channel is marked, at least during the season, with buoys laid by the HMYC. The direction from the fairway buoy is presently approximately 220°.

All moorings dry so it's likely only vessels which can take the ground will give Tetney consideration. However, the YC will welcome those who do and members are a source of valuable local knowledge.
www.humbermouthyachtclub.co.uk

The moorings are protected by a sand bank, known locally as The Whaleback, which makes for less bumping when grounding and re-floating. Picking up an available mooring is acceptable but do not leave your boat unattended without contacting the club.

The haven southeast of the clubhouse, important in the days of navigation to , is now not recommended. Obstructions abound, including substantial stone training walls which cover with the tide.

Facilities and visitor information

During the sailing season, HMYC provides showers, toilets and cooking facilities and everything else one would expect from a friendly sailing club. Within easy walking distance is the Haven Thorpe Park Holiday Centre where provisions and gas are obtainable. For more bucolic entertainment, the RSPB Tetney Marshes Reserve nearby can be home to over 30,000 wading birds at certain times of year.

Grimsby

The largest conurbation in northeast Lincolnshire, Grimsby is a study in fluctuating industrial fortunes. From a position as home to the world's largest fishing fleet until around 1950, there is now no fish landed locally and fishing's sudden demise brought an end to a way of life of generations. But Grimsby has not stood still. The town today has the largest fish market in the UK but the product is brought in by road.

The fish market, built in 1996 and upgraded in 2012, is one of the most important in Europe. Trading can go on 24 hours a day, all year round. And it is Grimsby Fish Dock Enterprises which manage the dock and access through the lock. Fish processing continues, with 70% of the UK's such industry in the town. And though the dock estate is sadly underdeveloped, many artisan fish businesses trade here in an area known as The Kasbah. In 2009, Grimsby smoked fish was awarded Protected Geographical status by the EU.

Grimsby is home to around 500 food related processing companies making it one of Europe's largest centres for food manufacturing, research, storage and distribution. And where is it that more electricity is generated from solar, wind, biomass and land fill gas than anywhere else in England? Yes, Grimsby.

The enclosed dock complex dating from the late 18th century remains active for general cargo and the No.2 Fish Dock is managed by the Humber Cruising Association as a marina. The Grimsby and Cleethorpes Yacht Club is based through Royal Dock, where Union Dock meets Alexandra Dock and both organisations welcome visitors.

Approaches and entry

From seaward

Whether arriving from the south or north, having Grimsby as a destination means a final approach on the south side of the estuary, following the charted small craft and wind farm transfer vessel recommended route. From the 4B PHM Fl.R.2s, a course due west generally finds the deepest water through the final 2.5M to the lock complex. The splendid 61m high Grimsby Dock Tower, despite earlier threats to demolish it, will almost certainly be the clearest visual reference on the shore.

Any refinement over charted depth here can be found from the latest ABP survey of Grimsby River Terminal. As a further visual guide, if entering via the Fish Docks lock, the tower will be left well to starboard. If entering

Useful information – Grimsby

ABP chart agents B.Cooke & Son Ltd ☏ + 44 1482 224412, www.bcookeandson.co.uk
Kildale Marine Ltd ☏ + 44 1482 227464, www.kildalemarine.co.uk

Fairway buoy Nearest equivalent is Lower Burcom LF Fl.R 4s in position 53°35′·39N 000°01′·73W

Buoyed channel From seaward, follow recommended route/s for small craft. From up river, inside Burcom Sand is an option depending on draught and height of tide. Otherwise to south side of main buoyed channel to Grimsby Road. Main visual reference is Grimsby Dock Tower.

Moorings All afloat pontoon moorings in one of two locked docks. Humber Cruising Association (HCA) in Fish Dock No. 2 OR Grimsby & Cleethorpes YC (G&CYC) in Royal Dock complex. HCA is the more usual option for the short term, casual visitor. (See main text). Full shoreside facilities.

Mooring enquiries to HCA www.hcagrimsby.co.uk OR for G&CYC winshipsimon@gmail.com

Contacts ABP contact via email or VTS on VHF.
HCA ☏ +44 1472 268428 or ☏ +44 7415 209659
G&CYC ☏ +44 7718 159599

Harbour Authority Associated British Ports (ABP) Humber. www.humber.com

VHF Port Working Channel Channel 12 in Grimsby sector. Lock Keepers Channel 74 'Fish Dock Island' OR 'Royal Dock.'

Tidal predictions based on Immingham.

Hazards Final approach to Fish Dock lock is shoal. Custom and practice is to time arrival over lock free flow period. For Fish Dock HW +/-2hrs. Royal Dock HW −1.5hr/HW. Royal Dock has much commercial ship traffic especially over free flow period. Early liaison with either lock on VHF is recommended.

Charts Admiralty 1188 Spurn Head to Immingham, ABP Spurn to Barton Haven, Imray C29

Norfolk, The Wash and Humber

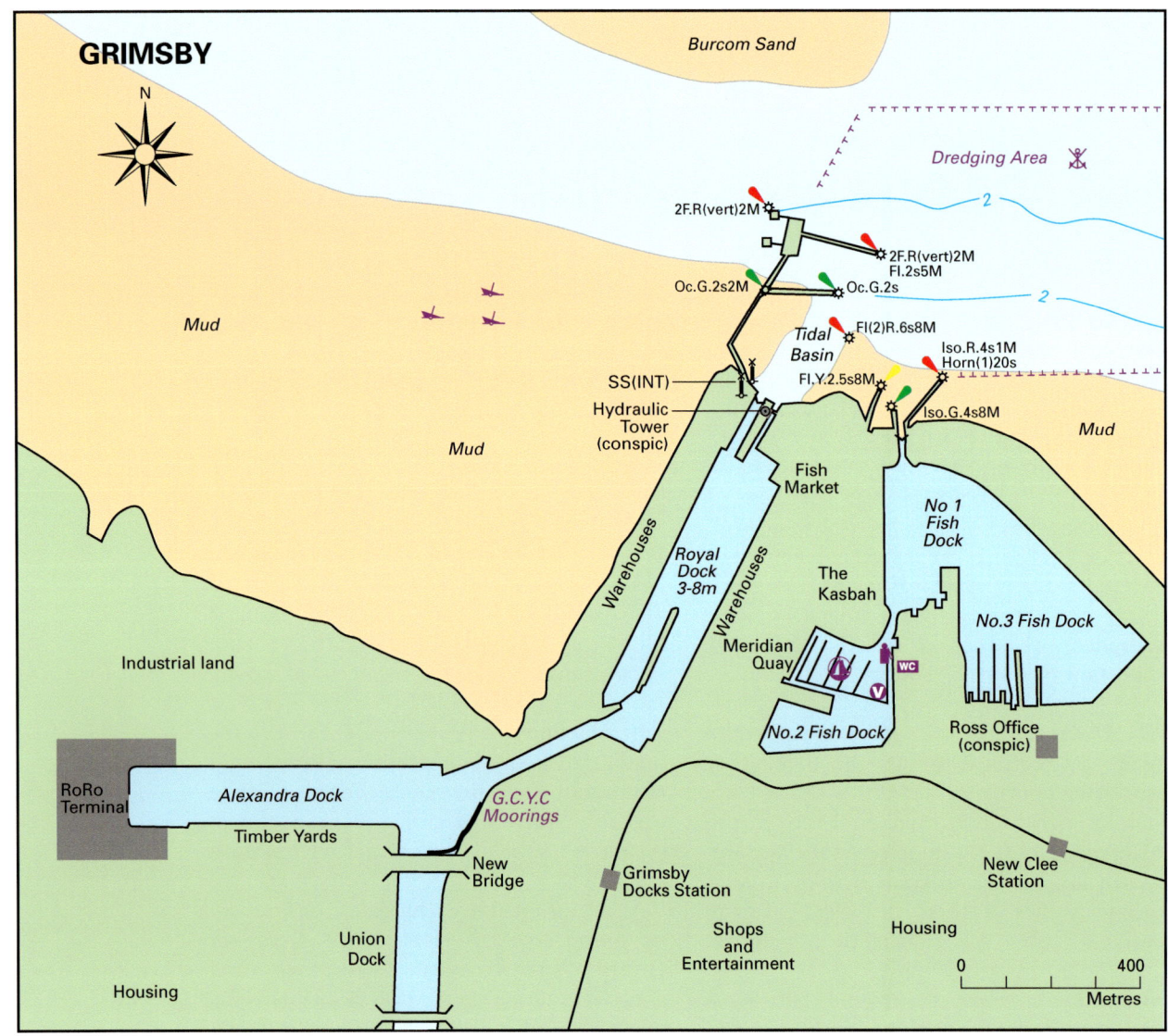

the Royal Dock, the tower will be left close to port. In either case, ensure early contact on VHF 74. Call Fish Dock Island or Royal Dock accordingly who will also give a tide gauge reading on request.

From up Humber

Once past Immingham Dock, the mariner will doubtless have taken station towards the south and if preferring deeper water, the line of Upper Burcom (Fl. (2) R.6s) to the edge of Stallingborough Flat is the desired course. The disadvantage of this, if the passage is on the ebb, is that to remain in deeper water, it will be necessary to delay turning towards the lock entrance until Lower Burcom (PHM Fl. R. 4s) from where the final run in will be against the tide.

The 'tiger line', as golfers will know it, will be across Burcom Shoal, inside Burcom Sand where charted depths are significantly less.

From Upper Burcom PHM, a course made good of 130° for approximately 3.5M will serve. This option will depend on draught, height of tide and sea state. Planning should start with the latest ABP Humber survey chart 'Grimsby to Immingham' which can be viewed on their website.

www.humber.com/Estuary_information

If this short cut is preferred, be aware that passage is prohibited between the Humber Power intake diffusers. These are positioned towards the buoyed channel so should not come into play. They have PH topmarks which are lit.

Fish Dock and Marina

Lock dimensions: Length 73m. Width 12.8m. Depth 5.5m. Maximum vessel length for penning 28m Marine Control VHF 74. 'Fish Dock Island.' ☎ +44 1472 267240. Free flow HW +/-2h. If access is required outside the free flow period, discuss in advance with Marine Control as draught and tidal height will have a bearing on timings.

Optimum time for arrival varies. For the Fish Dock and marina, free flow is HW +/-2h. Outside these times, and depending on tidal height, vessels can be penned (locked) in or out, but for a charge (£20.00 each way at time of writing) collected along with mooring fees at the marina. However, final approaches to the lock can dry so arrival time is restricted.

Royal Dock and GCYC

Lock dimensions: Length (maximum vessel size) 82.5m. Width 20.6m. Lock office on VHF 74 'Royal Dock.' ☎ +44 1472 2446233. Free flow HW -1.5h / HW. Penning is possible outside the free flow period, by arrangement and with 48 hours notice. Any vessel planning an entry over the free flow period needs to be aware that this could coincide with ship movements. Therefore, local liaison in advance is essential.

For the Royal Dock, if visiting the Grimsby & Cleethorpes YC, free flow is HW -1.5h/HW, before and after which times penning in or out can be arranged. Depths in the tidal basin are less restricted.

Call ahead on VHF 74 for either Fish Dock Island or Royal Dock, no later than the Lower Burcom PHM or equivalent distance if from up Humber. Being appraised of other vessel movements is very important. The Royal Dock complex handles deep sea vessels. The Fish Dock is home to high speed wind farm service craft. Arriving unannounced at either is imprudent. Comply with International Port Traffic Signals when entering locks.

Moorings

For the cruising sailor, the facilities managed by the Humber Cruising Association will doubtless be the objective. Their moorings for visitors are to the East Quay, found directly ahead from the lock in Fish Dock No.2, immediately beyond the fuel berth.

For enquiries regarding visitor mooring contact the Berthmaster ☎ +44 1472 268428 Mobile ☎ +44 7415 209659, 0800-1600, 7 days. Mooring fees are relatively modest. £2.30/m per night. (Minimum 7m). £10.50/m per week. £28.50/m per month. £66.00/m per three months maximum. Electricity included in single day rate. Otherwise charged as used.

There is commercial quay space available with power and water in Fish Dock No.1,

Grimsby hydraulic tower and lock to Royal Dock
Mark Ashley Miller

adjacent to the fish market and immediately to starboard after clearing the lock. Small commercial vessels can be accommodated in Fish Dock No.3 where Grimsby Shipyard Services Ltd. have a 200 tonne boat lift for vessels up to 11.5m beam.
☎ +44 1472 350023.

The Grimsby & Cleethorpes Yacht Club (G&CYC) have moorings where Union Dock meets Alexandra Dock in the west dock complex. Entry is via Royal Dock and its separate lock. These docks have busy commercial quaysides and the RoRo berth is a major conduit for car importation.

The G&CYC is welcoming but is not geared to the casual visitor. A distant yacht club seeking a destination for a rally is a different matter, as would be a solitary cruiser wanting temporary membership for an extended period. For such purposes, speak with the Moorings Officer on
☎ +44 7718 159599.
Email winshipsimon@gmail.com

Facilities

The HCA shoreside facilities are on East Quay, as is the 35 tonne boat lift. A modern clubhouse with showers and toilets is here too.

In that Grimsby is home to many small commercial vessels, the attendant trades for maintenance and repair are pretty much all on hand or readily available. Sadly, a chandler is no longer nearby but there are two in Hull and they will send what's required in short order. For any visiting yacht requiring repair therefore, Grimsby can serve well and there is plenty of advice and direction to be found. No substitute for local knowledge.

The town centre is a longer walk than ideal, but all that could be wanted by way of provisions can be readily found and taxis are used to the needs of visiting sailors.

The restaurant scene is a mixture of independent and chain and there is no shortage of choice. And don't forget the artisanal fish businesses in the nearby Kasbah. Visiting Grimsby and not sampling the smoked fish would be a travesty.

The railway station is close by with links to local places of interest as well as those further afield. Sheffield, for example, or the cathedral city of Lincoln and even cross country to Manchester. Enquire at the local tourist information centre in the Fishing Heritage Centre nearby. More than worthy of a visit in its own right it tells the story of a remarkable way of life and there is even a preserved fishing vessel, the 'Ross Tiger' to explore.
www.fishingheritage.com

Upriver from Grimsby

Sailing above the Humber bridge has a certain caché and South Ferriby, with its non-tidal moorings and a Michelin Guide rated riverside pub, is a tempting prospect. But Grimsby pier heads to Ferriby Sluice is approximately 21M which could be too far on one tide, given locking restrictions at both ends, particularly if the passage is for the first time. More manageable is Hull Marina (14M) with a HW +/- 3hr window to lock in, though best to aim for arrival close to HW to avoid the worst of the flow past the Hull lock basin entrance, particularly if constrained by boat speed.

Leave Grimsby during the free flow period before local HW to carry the flood upstream. Depending on your draught and the height of tide, this usually gives the option of a course over Burcom Shoal and Stallingborough Flat before crossing the main shipping channel to the Yorkshire side off Paull Sand and on into Hull Road. Time of HW at Hull Albert Dock is approximately +30 minutes on Grimsby so the passage is achievable.

From Hull, other upstream destinations become manageable, even allowing for tidal constraints.

Stone Creek Sunk Island *Trevor Doyle*

Stone Creek

Some of the smaller creeks and havens around the Humber are better considered as an esoteric category and if one must knock them off *'because they're there'*, do it with forethought and the benefit of local knowledge. Maybe Stone Creek is one of these.

On the north shore opposite Immingham, so named because it was once where stone was landed to form a bridge to the mainland, Stone Creek remains home to a few local boats. It dries completely.

Interesting in this vicinity is the phenomenon of Sunk Island, an example of natural land reclamation. In the reign of Charles I, an accretion of sand began which, over time, has resulted in a land mass of over 11,000 acres of mainly rich and fertile agricultural soils. At the last count, it was also home to some 228 souls. Because this land emerged from the sea bed, it remains a Crown Estate village where stands the parish church of Holy Trinity. One can but hope that rising sea levels will not reverse the process.

Villages with further facility are some 6 miles or more away, but adjacent is Stone Creek Campsite welcoming caravans, tents and motorhomes amid a rural idyl of coastal walks and wildlife.

For mariners wanting to know more of Stone Creek and access by boat, the local contacts are the Chairman of the boat club on ☎ +44 1964 631814 and the Harbourmaster on ☎ +44 7894 705168.

Skitter Haven (East Halton Skitter)

Continuing from Immingham up the Lincolnshire shore, Skitter Haven sits less than 2M south-southeast of Skitter Ness. Like other such tidal inlets, Skitter is perhaps best left to those with local knowledge or an urge to, like Greta Garbo, be alone. But this writer would be the last to decry the tranquillity of such rural idylls, particularly in the right weather when, with glass in hand and the curlew for company, all would be right with the world.

Entry

Accessed across Halton Flat from the buoyed channel it actually boasts the eponymous PHM, Skitter Haven Fl.R.4s from which the creek is due west. Shore beacons immediately north of the opening mark a cross estuary gas pipeline.

The haven itself dries from at least half tide, is not surveyed routinely, has no mooring unless one wishes to lie alongside the sluice structure at the inward end, and the village of East Halton, despite the attraction of the Black Bull PH is a two-mile walk.

However, if you are in a small boat which can take the ground and you are bound up river late on the tide, especially with testing weather from the west, rather than round Skitter Ness the haven could provide respite until the next tide serves.

Anchorage

If constrained by draught or not having the benefit of twin keels, there is a safe anchorage to be had by laying off south of the haven between the Humber Sea Terminal and Skitter, riverward of the 2m contour. The brickyard chimney across Halton Flat is a conspicuous landmark.

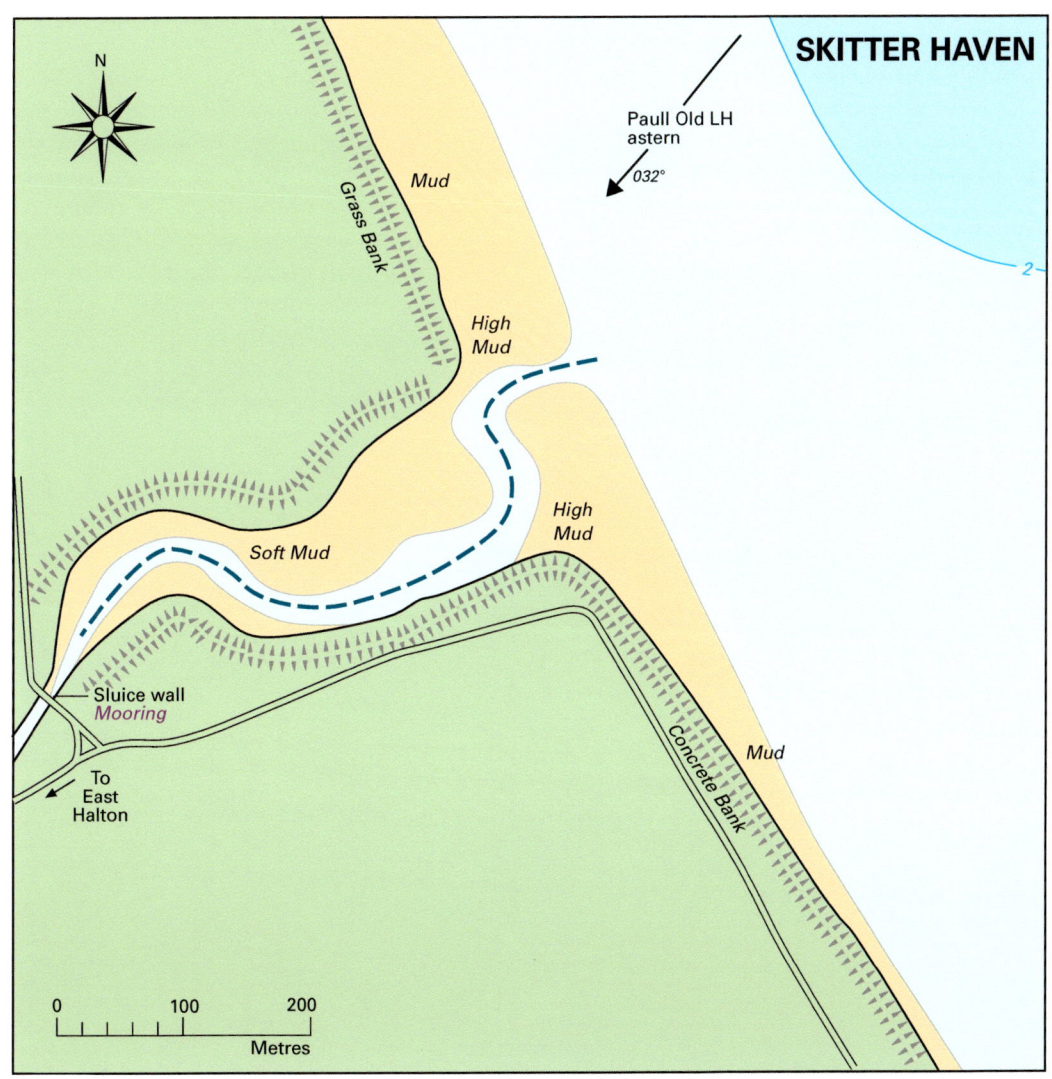

Facilities

The small village of East Halton is some two miles from the haven and its population is under 700. It nonetheless has St. Peter's church, a shop, post office and the Black Bull Inn which enjoys a good, local reputation for its food and accommodation.

Hedon

On the Yorkshire shore, immediately below King George and Queen Elizabeth Docks in Hull and downstream of Paull, lies Saltend Jetty, behind which is Hedon Haven. Once of great significance, Hedon Haven allowed ships to unload in Hedon Itself, the busiest port around from as early as the 12th century until Hull took over.

As an inland port, Hedon did survive until 1970 but a combination over time of the railways, siltation, Hull Docks and ship size finally did for it. Given the industrial nature of the immediate vicinity, comprised mostly of Saltend Chemicals Park and the power station, as well as more than 3.5m drying heights before one can enter the haven proper, it does beg the question as to why one would venture in.

The haven now is officially only that which remains tidal. Hedon town retains previously canalised sections which constituted the earlier port facility.

Plans apparently exist for a revival of the haven as a leisure waterway, with a marina and country park south of Hedon. There is an argument for allowing this to come to fruition before paying a visit, no disrespect intended.

Further upstream is the village of Paull, close to 19A SHM. Identified by the disused fort, lighthouse and the St. Andrew's church tower it too offers shelter from the north.

Hull

More properly Kingston-upon-Hull, the city stands on the River Hull at its confluence with The Humber. Its prosperity was built on seafaring and its attendant trades, first whaling and then commercial fishing. Begun in the 12th century, Hull's major export became wool and later, as part of the Hanseatic League, wool products and the import of wine and timber added to its economic fortunes.

After the English Civil War, dock construction began and continued into the mid-1800s. Whaling was prominent until its eventual decline in the 19th century and as sail gave way to steam, Hull's sphere of influence widened to serve the southern hemisphere frozen meat trade. It also had prominence in the inland and coastal shipping network.

Tranquil mooring in Hull

Hull

Up until the First World War, Hull was a conduit for emigrants from northern Europe who crossed to Liverpool before setting sail for the New World. This move into passenger shipping spawned the Wilson Line which by the early 20th century was the largest privately owned line in the world. It was later sold to become part of Ellerman Lines, also owned by a Hull shipping magnate.

Prosperity continued until just before the First World War and in 1897 city status was granted. After the decline of whaling, attention turned to deep sea fishing which was a staple until the 1975-6 'Cod Wars,' the settlement of which initiated Hull's downturn. Despite this, Hull is twinned with, amongst other places, Reykjavik.

All things being cyclical, 21st century Hull is a thriving conurbation of over 250,000 inhabitants and a broad range of industries. The university was founded in 1927 and the Hull School of Art is respected internationally. In 2017, Hull was appointed UK City of Culture and the positive impacts of that status continue to be felt.

Useful information – Hull

Fairway buoy Hull Marina outer, tidal basin is 3+ cables NWbyW of Upper West Middle No. 26 PHM Fl.R 4s. River Hull tidal barrier (30m conspic.) 1.5 cables downstream of basin pier heads.

Buoyed channel Hull Road is the well defined, buoyed channel to the north bank.

Moorings Hull Marina. Modern marina with all afloat pontoon berths in locked basin. Full marina facilities. Boatyard. Chandlery. City centre within walking distance.

Contacts ABP contact by email www.humber.com
Hull Marina ☏ +44 1482 609960.
Duty Lock Keeper ☏ +44 7789 178501
Harbour Authority Associated British Ports (ABP).

VHF Port Working Channel VHF 12 in the Hull sector. Inter-ship VHF 10. Marina Lock VHF 80.

Tidal predictions based on Hull (Albert Dock).

Inland waterways access 16 miles of navigation on the River Hull for suitable boats.

Hazards Commercial vessel traffic through Hull Roads. Rate of tidal flow even over HW. Lock access is HW +/- 3 hrs. Outer basin can dry. Lock sill is 2m above CD. Pre-book berth during peak season.

Charts Admiralty 1188. Imray C29. ABP Spurn to Barton Haven and others of larger scale. See website www.humber.com

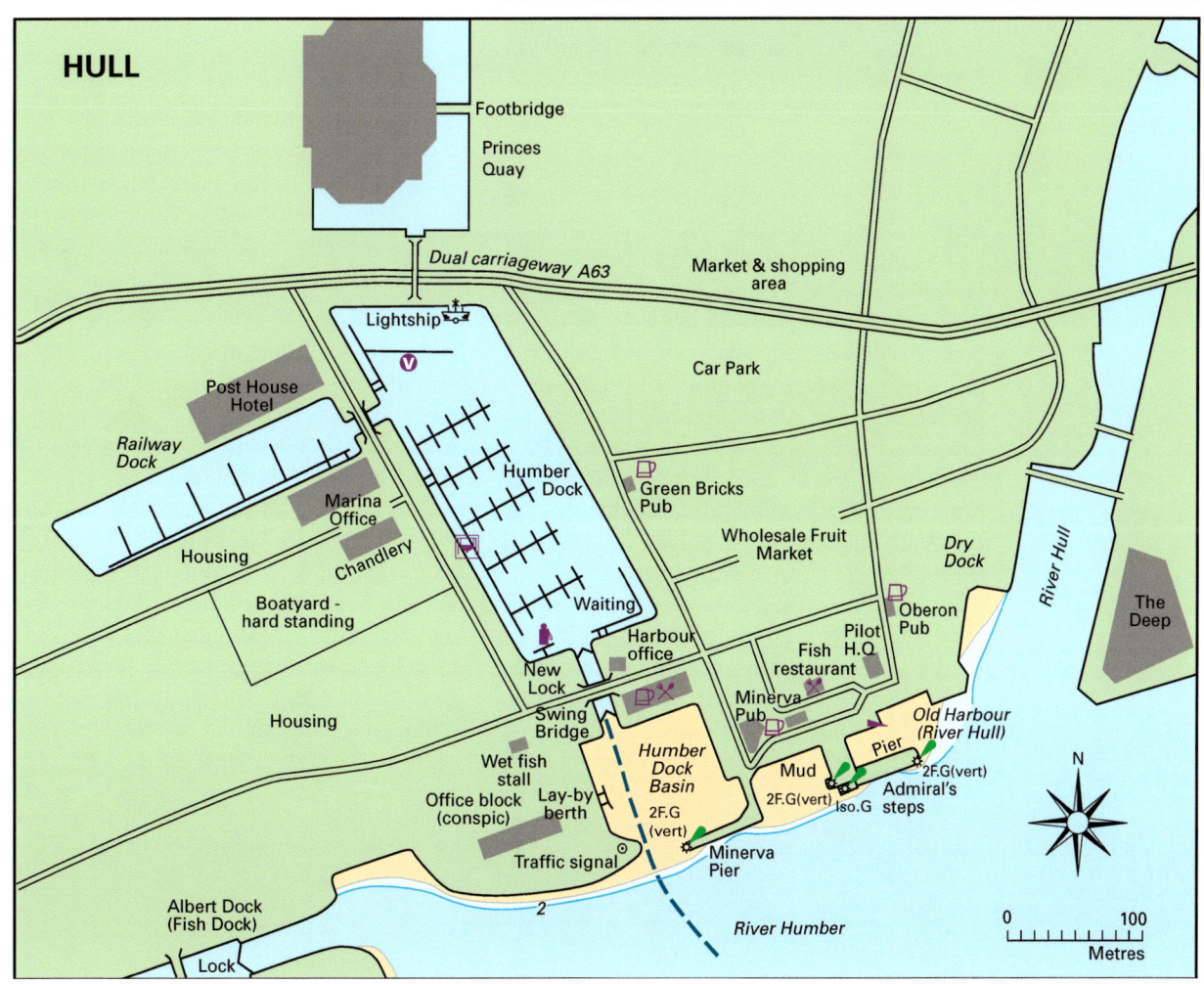

Hull and the sea

Hull Marina is a 'not to be missed' destination for any yacht visiting the Humber. Mooring here, with all it offers, will not disappoint.

Approaches

Heading upstream, gaining Hull Roads is straightforward through the buoyed channel past Paull. As it sweeps around to the west, Hull Roads is well buoyed and offers ample deep water at all states of the tide. Principal concerns then will be commercial ship movements (which monitor VHF 12) and, potentially, tidal set around the bight. Rates can be over 3 kts even close to the time of HW.

From upstream and once through the Humber Bridge, Hull Middle, which dries is the main concern but the passage is clear and the ABP chart Hessle Sand refers.

Landmarks on final approach are the River Hull tidal surge barrier (30m high) followed by the stylised aquarium building known as The Deep. Immediately upstream of the marina is a modern office block with much glass. The lock is inward of a tidal basin, access to which is between offset pierheads.

The lock to Hull Marina is a 24 hour operation but access HW +/3 hrs on Albert Dock. The lock cill is 2m above chart datum.

On the port hand inside the pierheads is a temporary mooring staging for use outside lock opening times. However, the basin is heavily silted and can dry over LWS. Seek guidance from the duty lock keeper on VHF 80 or ☎ +44 7789 178501. The main telephone number for the marina is ☎ +44 1482 609960 but at times this can lead to a recorded response.

The lock is controlled with International Port Traffic Signals.

Moorings

Hull Marina is, by any standard, a fine facility, with everything you might expect from a modern marina. Now part of the Aquavista Group, there can be cross benefits for those in the 'family.' Four TYHA Gold Anchors proclaim the standard. For those who live by Facebook and Twitter, there are the inevitable links. More than 200 permanent, pontoon berths include ample provision for visitors, but pre-booking is advisable at peak times.

Unless directed otherwise, a turn to starboard once through the lock, then to port, then ahead for the whole length of the marina will bring you to the dedicated visitor berths alongside a footbridge of futuristic design.

Facilities

From a specific small craft perspective, there are all the marine trades and two chandleries, one alongside the marina, as is the marina office in the traditional, red brick warehouse to the NW corner. Fuel, pump out, free WiFi, laundry and a 50 tonne boat hoist.

Undoubtedly, the strength of Hull Marina is its proximity to the city centre. This coupled with the adjacent waterfront development means that, if one were so inclined, even an extended stay in Hull could be enjoyed without venturing far at all. Most gastronomic tastes are catered for and in addition to the familiar names, independent options abound, on and off the beaten track.

Hull Marina and the new footbridge into the city

The striking aquarium building, The Deep, immediately downstream of the lock basin *A G Baxter / Shutterstock.com*

Norfolk, The Wash and Humber

Visitor information

A short walk via the funky footbridge leads to the city proper with its mix of new and older architecture. Hull was affected considerably by wartime bombing and its buildings reflect this.

Hull does not want for things happening. Given no outside adverse influences, a festival season awaits, catering for all comers. Classical music to jazz to Heavy Metal to comedy.

The maritime museum tells a long and important local story and two theatres offer varied programmes. The Ferens Art Gallery has hosted the Turner Prize.

The poetry tradition is strong, Philip Larkin being a famous son of Hull. Others claimed as 'Hullensians' include William Wilberforce and Amy Johnson.

New Holland

Until 1803, this location was but a creek, approximately opposite Hull, which spawned a ferry service around 1825. It is nonetheless suggested this was just a front for illicit gin imports from the Netherlands, which gave rise to the local place name.

The Humber bridge did for the ferry and the pier was acquired by New Holland Bulk Services. Today it is the HES Humber Bulk Terminal, part of HES International, a group with firm Dutch roots. Handling dry bulk cargoes, they make no mention of gin, but who knows?

New Holland Dock is the operator of the basin and adjacent quay, another dry cargo handling facility receiving ships up to 5000 dwt.

The net result is despite New Holland's historic advantage for the small boat sailor, for all practical purposes this is no longer an option. For those in pursuit of the area's maritime heritage, it is best sought from landward.

Barrow-upon-Humber

The region covered by this pilot has many a claim to fame if one is prepared to look a little harder and Barrow-upon-Humber is no exception. For it was home for a significant part of his life to a man who changed the world. That man was carpenter and self-taught clockmaker John Harrison.

The resilience and accuracy of his clocks at sea solved the problem of longitude. He altered the face of navigation forever. And he did this despite considerable opposition and scorn when even the likes of Isaac Newton deemed it unlikely a sufficiently accurate timepiece would ever be built. So, if the pub quiz ever enquires as to what Westminster Abbey and Barrow-upon-Humber have in common, the answer is memorials to John Harrison. But how to make a pilgrimage to Barrow where traces of Harrison can still be seen?

Barrow Haven

Barrow-upon-Humber

Approaches

The Skitter Channel, running between Hull Middle and Hessle sands will likely, according to tide, be subject to commercial ship movements. Monitor VHF 12 and keep a good lookout, fore and aft. It is possible that a vessel up to 120m LOA could be inward to Barrow itself, as the wharf at the riverward end of the haven is very much a working one and handles considerable Baltic timber traffic. In fact, the stacks of timber are a good visual indication as to the location.

0.5M east of Barrow, and a prominent waymark, is Barrow House North chimney. Less than 0.2M downstream of the haven stands Barrow East chimney.

Those references apart, the opening is from approximately mid-way between No.22A PHM Fl.R.2s and No.28A PHM Fl.R.4s, across Barton Ness Sand where drying heights vary up to 2m.

Entry

The haven itself is efficiently scoured courtesy of the tidal barrier and sluice from which water is periodically released, but there is significant siltation to both banks. This can be particularly so at the entrance where a course perpendicular to the main river bank should be the aim rather than cutting the corners.

The deepest water is found in the centre of the channel but it is not unusual for there to be vessels, some relatively large, moored in such a way as to obstruct the fairway. While the bottom is generally soft mud, unless entry is over a HW period, grounding is a distinct possibility. Note that the railway bridge immediately upstream of the mooring staging is not something to encounter without having control.

John Harrison, the man who changed the world

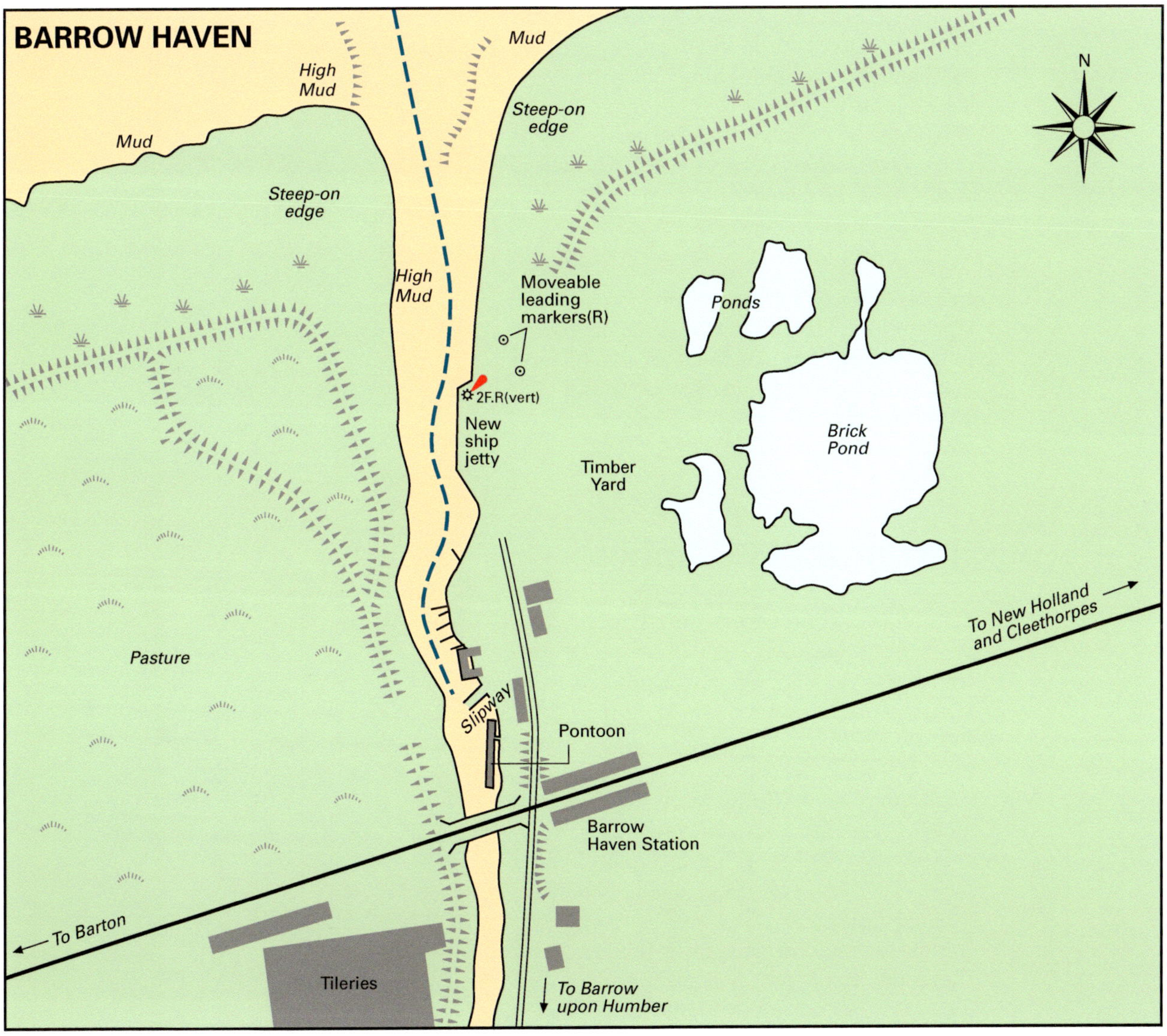

Moorings

Moorings do exist but all dry of course and consist of wooden staging of various vintages. Casual mooring is not generally catered for but enquiry in advance can be made of William Foster & Sons who own and manage most of them ☎ +44 1469 530667. In extremis, and as long as there is not a ship on the commercial berth, the good people of Old Ferry Wharf are amenable to providing a safe haven and over a tide, but only that ☎ +44 1469 533335.

Facilities

At one time, the immediate area alongside the river had over twenty brickyards and tileries and this is reflected in the buildings hereabouts. However, there is little available in the immediate vicinity to satisfy the leisure sailor's requirements. It will be necessary to look slightly further afield. To this end, the adjacent railway line served by Barrow Haven station has services to Grimsby and Cleethorpes to the east and Barton-upon-Humber to the west. Two hourly service (0620 to 2150). Alternatively, a bus service joins nearby towns and villages including Barrow itself. The village is close to a three mile walk from the haven.

Visitor information

In Holy Trinity Church, a display explains the work of John Harrison and a statue of him sits in the village centre. Barrow is an architectural gem and its buildings, market place and high street are as fine as you could wish for.
www.barrow-upon-humber.co.uk

Barton-upon-Humber

Continuing upstream from Barrow, the aesthetic appeal of the Humber Bridge transforms the outlook as you proceed west. If navigating beyond the bridge, then after Barrow the buoyed channel falls away from the south bank and continues between the two main, conspicuous bridge towers. The span is 1410m long with a vertical clearance of 30m.

Here the VHF working channel changes from VHF 12 to VHF 15 going west but VHF 10 intership.

Immediately downstream of the bridge on the south bank lies Barton-upon-Humber. This is the largest of the tidal haven settlements and one where an air of vibrancy and renewal prevails.

Despite the popular economic viewpoint that continuous growth is both possible and an entitlement, history shows that fortunes fluctuate and Barton is a case in point. To say it was once significant as a centre of local shipbuilding is an understatement. This in addition to tanning, malting, brick, tile, whiting and rope manufacturing, as well as three corn mills. The railway station is the terminus of the branch line from Grimsby and, before the bridge, ferry services for passengers and freight once plied several times a day to and from Hessel and Hull.

But times change. Trading vessels of the 19th century are now, if they're lucky, on the National Register of Historic Vessels. 90% of

Waters' Edge Visitor Centre. Unmistakable landmark

Barton haven looking riverward at low water

what we consume goes by road and, before that, the coming of the railways had its adverse effect on Barton shipbuilding too. Some adapted though. Clapson & Sons built leisure craft, latterly even in GRP as well as fishing vessels in steel and in the Second World War, minesweepers and MFVs for the Admiralty. The Humber has a proud record in minesweeping, as the memorial near Royal Dock Tower in Grimsby attests.

Come 2021, a healthy revival was clearly in evidence. Joe Irving at Barton Haven Boatyard again continues the maritime trades tradition, offering building and repair services for leisure and small commercial vessels.

Approaches

Barton Haven entry is 0.2M east of the Humber Bridge. Entry around local HW is recommended but can be earlier according to draught. The inter-tidal area of Barton Ness Sand dries to 2m above chart datum and in places more, and extends 0.1M riverward. Both banks of the haven are sheet piled and form a natural bell mouth. On the downstream corner stands the Waters' Edge Visitor Centre, a highly stylised, low building with a sloping roof, seen as pale green from the river. To the upstream side is a small wooded area and, on the flood wall, a red brick building which once housed the coastguard, now the Viking Way Café. The charted feature extending riverward from

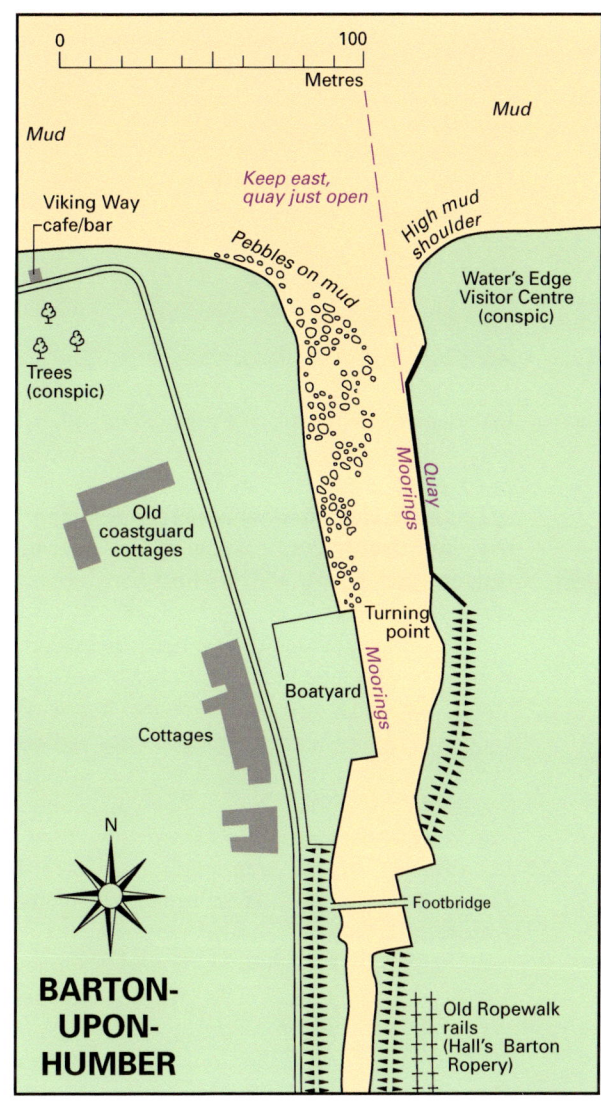

Barton haven inward. Water to the port hand

Norfolk, The Wash and Humber

Part of Barton's maritime heritage

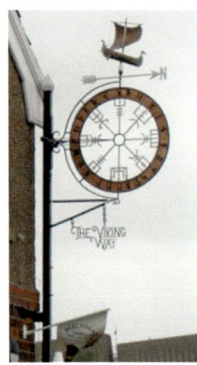

147 miles to go on the Viking Way!

here depicts the location of the old coastguard jetty but little or no sign remains even when uncovered.

The approach channel is perpendicular to the river bank but narrow. Keep to the downstream piling wall to find the deepest water.

Immediately inside the haven, the upstream bank is heavily silted and a number of vessels, some large, are aground here for much of each tide. Once the east bank becomes a grass covered incline, the channel veers gently to starboard and Barton Haven Boatyard comes into view, with moorings off it. Arrangements in advance are recommended. All yard moorings dry into a soft, muddy bottom. Mooring in the stream and securing to the west bank will be on harder ground. Contact Joe Irving ☎ +44 7919 877405 who is welcoming and accommodating.

Once past the yard the channel degenerates into an overgrown stream and a footbridge with limited headroom crosses between the banks.

Facilities and visitor information

All that could reasonably be required is within easy walking distance. A large supermarket and the railway station are closest, and the town centre not far beyond. The town demonstrates a pride in its heritage and The Ropewalk gallery and exhibition space is also a venue for the performing arts, an artists' studio and museum.
www.roperyhall.co.uk
www.the-ropewalk.co.uk

Walk to the river on the east bank and the Waters' Edge Visitor Centre is a hive of activity as well as offering a view of the river and bridge from a position of comfort. ☎ +44 1642 631500. Nearby is the Far Ings National Nature Reserve formed of former clay workings alongside the river. No shortage of pubs in Barton either. At least seven at the last count.
www.barton-upon-humber.co.uk

Whatever your vessel's draught, Barton-upon-Humber is, like other locations, worth exploring and doing so from landward is straightforward. If, for example, your boat is in Grimsby, travelling along the south bank by public transport represents an eminently workable option. By train or bus, or a combination of both, nothing need be missed and much gained.

Hessle

Saxons then the Viking invaders used this haven *en route* to York, but these days the prospect is less inviting.

Hessle Haven was once the Yorkshire end of the Humber Ferry to and from Barton. But when the service ended, so too did one reason for the haven to exist. Coupled with the demise of shipbuilding, evident here since the 17th century and continuing until 1994, the haven, which gave rise to the town of Hessle, now presents as something of a wasted waterfront development opportunity. This despite the siltation and the industrial aspect on the downstream side.

Even recently there were small boats moored to staging here which made for shoreside access but they seem to have disappeared. And the Ferry Boat Inn, latterly an Italian restaurant has also fallen victim to something.

Fleet Drain runs through the haven, scouring a gutway down the centre and to one side is a built quay beyond which lies a trailer and container park and a car supermarket depot. On the other, an attractive wooded area and the Hessle Skatepark but no civilised means of getting ashore.

The siltation is extreme so that even drying out here could make for an uncomfortable time. We can but hope for change but in the meantime, there are preferable alternatives.

The story of Hessle is well worth following and between the Hull Maritime Museum ('*Stuffed to the gills with maritime artefacts*' according to Lonely Planet) and the Ferens Art Gallery, losing oneself in the archives for half a day or more would not be difficult. But first, find a berth in Hull Marina.

South Ferriby final approach looking riverward

Ferriby Sluice and South Ferriby

South Ferriby is a very adequate haven where a boat can be left on all afloat moorings on the non-tidal side of the sea lock. Even if you venture no further upstream than here, there is much to be enjoyed from having included Ferriby Sluice in your itinerary.

Situated where the River Ancholme meets the Humber, South Ferriby presents an industrial face courtesy of the cement works. It has, nevertheless, a bucolic countenance which easily deflects any sense of being back along the Immingham shore.

The River Ancholme runs north from its source, slightly less than 20 miles into Lincolnshire. It has seen various uses over many centuries and remains important as a drainage channel and for abstraction for industrial and agricultural purposes. All commercial use of the river ceased in the 1980s but there is considerable leisure use; fishing and boating and in Brigg, 8 miles upstream, there is a marina www.briggmarina.co.uk and the Glandford Boat Club which welcomes visitors. www.glandfordboatclub.org For those with the right boat, locking into the Ancholme offers a further destination to enhance a cruise itinerary.

Several bridges span the river, many of architectural significance. Few of them carry public roads now and have not therefore been replaced and along with Ferriby lock are either listed structures or scheduled ancient monuments. The river is also the home port of at least one historic vessel owned by the Humber Keel Preservation Society.
www.keelsandsloops.org.uk

> 'On the evening of February 25 1935 *Amy Howson* was expected at Ferriby Sluice from Hull on the way to Brigg with a cargo of seed for the Farmers Co Ltd. The lock keeper had left the lock ready for her arrival, but with a strong northerly breeze blowing straight into the haven, a rising tide and in full sail, *Amy's* crew would need to drop the sails and the mate get a rope on as she ran into the lock. Those who have sailed a Sloop will know that this meant several well-timed operations and some very fast 'nipping about' by both captain and mate, all to take place in about 100 yards and in the dark too! About 7pm there was a tap on the lock keeper's door, the door opened and in walked the captain of *Amy Howson*, Len Barraclough. He was rather upset and, before the lock keeper could speak, said: "I've hit the bridge and knocked a damn great piece out!" His mate had missed the bollard.
>
> Visibly shaken, the lock keeper leapt out of his chair, grabbed his jacket and torch and dashed for the door closely followed by Len. *Amy* was now lying clear of the bridge with a stop rope on, and in the light of the lock keepers torch a piece, some six feet long and 18 inches high, was missing from the outer girder of the cast iron bridge. Insults were exchanged between lock keeper and captain during a careful examination of the damage, after which it was declared safe to swing the bridge and pen *Amy* down into the Ancholme.
>
> Next morning *Amy* was away to Brigg, before the lock keeper could find any more to say on the subject. Later the bits of cast iron girder were recovered from the lock and the damage repaired by an engineer from Marshalls of Gainsborough.
>
> The outcome of this incident was that Lindsey County Council decided the bridge was no longer fit to take the ever-increasing road traffic and took over the task of providing a bridge at Ferriby Sluice. Later that year the old cast iron bridge, which had given 92 years of trouble-free service, was replaced by a new steel bridge, which ironically, never worked satisfactorily!'
>
> Reproduced by kind permission of the Humber Keel and Sloop Preservation Society

Charts

Given this destination is above the Humber Bridge, your usual charts may not suffice, their coverage ending at that point. If you are venturing west of the bridge you will require an Associated British Ports chart, at least that Barton Haven to Burton Stather. This is produced bi-monthly which gives an indication of the possible frequency of changes of depths.

Lock

As with any passage plan, working backwards makes sense and ascertaining available depth alongside, once though the lock, is a prudent beginning. River levels are not constant and vary according to a number of factors. Early contact with the lock keeper is advisable. Working hours for enquiry are 0800-1600 Monday to Sunday and 48 hours' notice for lock opening is the current requirement. The lock is owned and operated by the Environment Agency.

The lock chamber can accommodate vessels up to 20.5m LOA and 5.5m beam.

Least water on entry to the lock will vary according to height of tide. Lock keepers advise that a working level indication of 2.4m can be used for planning purposes but again, consulting in advance around a planned date and time of arrival is the safe basis for calculation. There is a tide gauge on approach.

Approaches

The first-time visitor in particular, will be best served inward and on the top of the tide. A flood, especially on springs, can produce a significant rate across the haven mouth, so arrival at or just before slack water has a number of advantages. The lock nonetheless will facilitate access approximately HW +/-2h.

Heading upstream towards the Humber Bridge, the prudent course is on the edge of the buoyed channel, maintaining awareness of commercial traffic and reporting to VTS Humber (VHF 15 inward). Working with the ABP chart, 'Barton Haven to Burton Stather', the recommended track is shown and marked by SHM No.27 Fl.G.2s below the bridge span and SHM No.29 Fl.G.4s above. This is also a good reporting point to 'South Ferriby Lock' on VHF 74.

From here, the adage that the deepest water is to the outside of a bend was never truer and it is tight into the south shore that the channel winds. So, from No.29 SHM, the required course becomes 225° to the next mark, PHM No.30 Fl.R.4s. A small course alteration from here onto 230° will bring up PHM No.32 Fl.R.2s. These compass courses can be important, particularly if visibility is poor as the marks are approximately 1M apart. Note too that charted depths in the buoyed channel when leaving the bridge astern are sufficient but not generous.

Closer now is SHM Lower Whitton Fl.(3)G.10s from where the inn on the downstream knuckle of the haven entrance becomes a landmark as does, more obviously, the cement works with its chimney behind the western extreme. Ahead will be Read's Island

The cement works and the lock gates at Ferriby Sluice

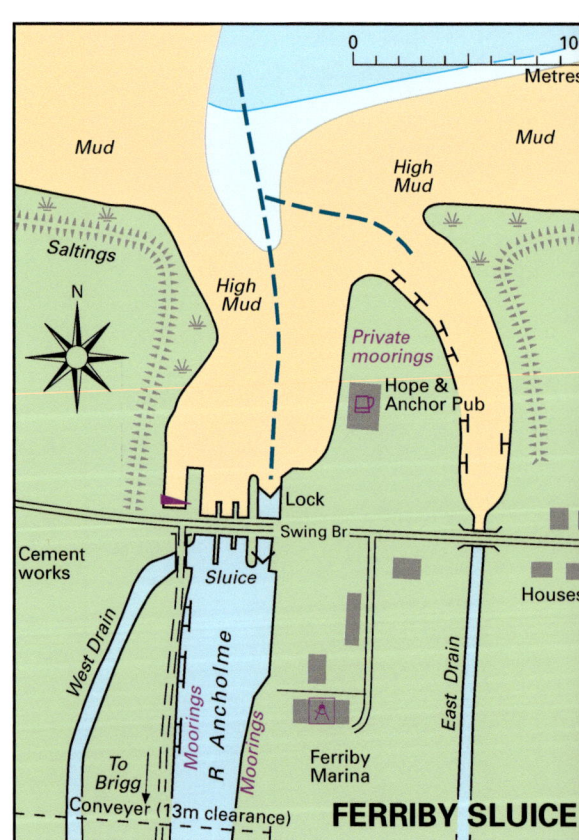

with PHM No.32A Fl.R.4s off its easternmost tip. There was a time when the channel behind the island was navigable but not now, so if you overshoot or prefer to ferry glide into the tide, it is the buoyed channel towards No.32A which offers an opportunity to turn.

The final approach should be with the haven fully open and the course due south. Do not cut the corner where there is considerable silting. The scour through the sluice or lock when fresh water is released maintains the depth but only to the centre line. Keep VHF contact with the lock keeper and do not proceed until instructed to do so. There is, after all, a road bridge for him to lift.

The lock chamber has wires running vertically. Run your mooring lines around these to accommodate the rise or fall of level.

Moorings

Once clear of the lock inbound, the principal moorings are on the port hand and it is possible the traditional Humber trading vessel, *Amy Howson* will be on her home berth. Beyond are the Environment Agency (EA) moorings which are without power and water but toilet facilities are immediately on the quayside.

Upstream of the EA moorings are serviced moorings owned and managed by South Ferriby Marina who also offer boat storage and chandlery.
☏ +44 1652 635620
www.southferribymarina.com

Useful information – South Ferriby and Ferriby Sluice

Fairway buoy Nearest equivalents are Lower Whitton LF Fl.(3)G 10s and No. 32A LF Fl R 4s.

Buoyed channel Between North and South Ferriby, above the bridge, the open width of the river is shoal and the principal, buoyed channel is tight into the south shore. Ferriby Sluice lies immediately east of Read's Island at the extreme of the bight. Cement works chimney is conspicuous.

Moorings All afloat alongside moorings in the basin at the mouth of the River Ancholme. South Ferriby Marina
☏ +44 1652 635620

Contacts ABP via email www.humber.com
Harbour Authority APB. For the lock and River Ancholme, the Environment Agency (EA).
Environment Agency www.huwww.gov.uk/guidance/river-ancholme-bridge-heights-locks-and-facilitiesmber.com ☏ +44 1653 635219

VHF Port Working Channel Channel 15 for this sector. South Ferriby Lock Channel 74.

Tidal predictions based on Hull (Albert Dock) N.B. A tide gauge is situated at South Ferriby where the time of HW is later than at Hull. Real time readings can be obtained from Humber VTS on VHF 15.

Inland waterways access River Ancholme to Brigg (8M) where marina facilities are available, mainly for powered craft and narrow boats. Air draught restrictions on this passage.

Hazards Final approach to the lock dries. Access is HW +/- 2hrs dependent on draught and tidal height. 48 hours notice required. Lock chamber is 20.5m LOA and 5.5m beam. Maximum draughts vary but in general 2.4m can be accommodated. Liaise with the lock keeper for topical information.

Charts Admiralty 3497 but for navigation above the Humber Bridge, the only charts showing soundings and buoyage are from Associated British Ports (ABP). For South Ferriby the chart Barton Haven to Burton Stather covers. Updated bi-monthly. See www.humber.com

Channel tight to the south shore upstream of the bridge

The traditional Humber trading vessel, *Amy Howson*, is one of the last of her kind

In the main, depths on all berths are approximately 2m/2.5m. Like the EA facilities, there is a concrete quay with wooden piles extending above the quay height in case of extreme river levels.

Upstream of these is a wooden staging, also owned by the marina, but to reach these it will be necessary to pass under the Ferriby Belt, the conveyer which serves the cement works. Published clearance is 13m but varies according to river level. Further upstream are electricity cables with a published 17.36m clearance, but check locally as they are believed to be lower. For clearances of all overhead obstructions, including bridges, consult the EA website.

According to the rules, any vessel entering EA waters requires a licence for the duration and this can be negotiated with the lock keeper once alongside. Locking is otherwise at no charge.

On the assumption entry has been less lively than that of the *Amy Howson*, you may notice, on final approach, the channel to the east and behind the inn where one or two boats are moored to staging. While this could be used in an emergency, it dries and a mooring there could not be guaranteed nor its provenance or condition vouched for.

Facilities

South Ferriby Marina is well equipped to cater for most small craft needs and has a well-stocked chandlery.

For the village of South Ferriby with all that villages offer, it will be necessary to walk just over half a mile east along the main road, A1077. Immediately across from the lock however is the Hope and Anchor PH which, from first impressions, appears like many a similar establishment offering what is affectionately termed 'pub grub'. Be not prejudiced however, as an early clue on approaching the front door is a little plaque bearing no less than the motif of Michelin Guide approval. But before regretting not to have packed the dinner jacket, note Michelin use 'rustic' in their description so the visitor here would be well advised to take advantage and never settle for less again. They even do takeaway and have rooms!
✆ +44 1652 635334
www.thehopeandanchorpub.co.uk

Winteringham Haven

A little over 2M upstream of Ferriby Sluice lies the entrance to Winteringham Haven. This is the last such tidal creek on the south shore before the Humber estuary becomes, at Apex Light, the Rivers Ouse and Trent. Long since a local destination for those with Grimsby or Hull as their home port, it is as different from either as could be imagined. A thousand souls at most live in the village nearby but is it on the road to nowhere? To think so is to do Winteringham an injustice:

Turn left out of Liverpool Street Station in London and you'll step onto Bishopsgate, as did the Romans but they called the highway Ermine Street. It took them via Lincoln to York. And, as was their habit, the road was dead straight. It still is, although we now give it a variety of numbers. But one thing hasn't changed. It arrives on the Humber estuary in Winteringham, from where the same Romans organised a ferry across to Brough.

The Domesday Book describes Winteringham as prosperous with three mills, a fishery and the ferry still there in 1086. In 1907 it gained

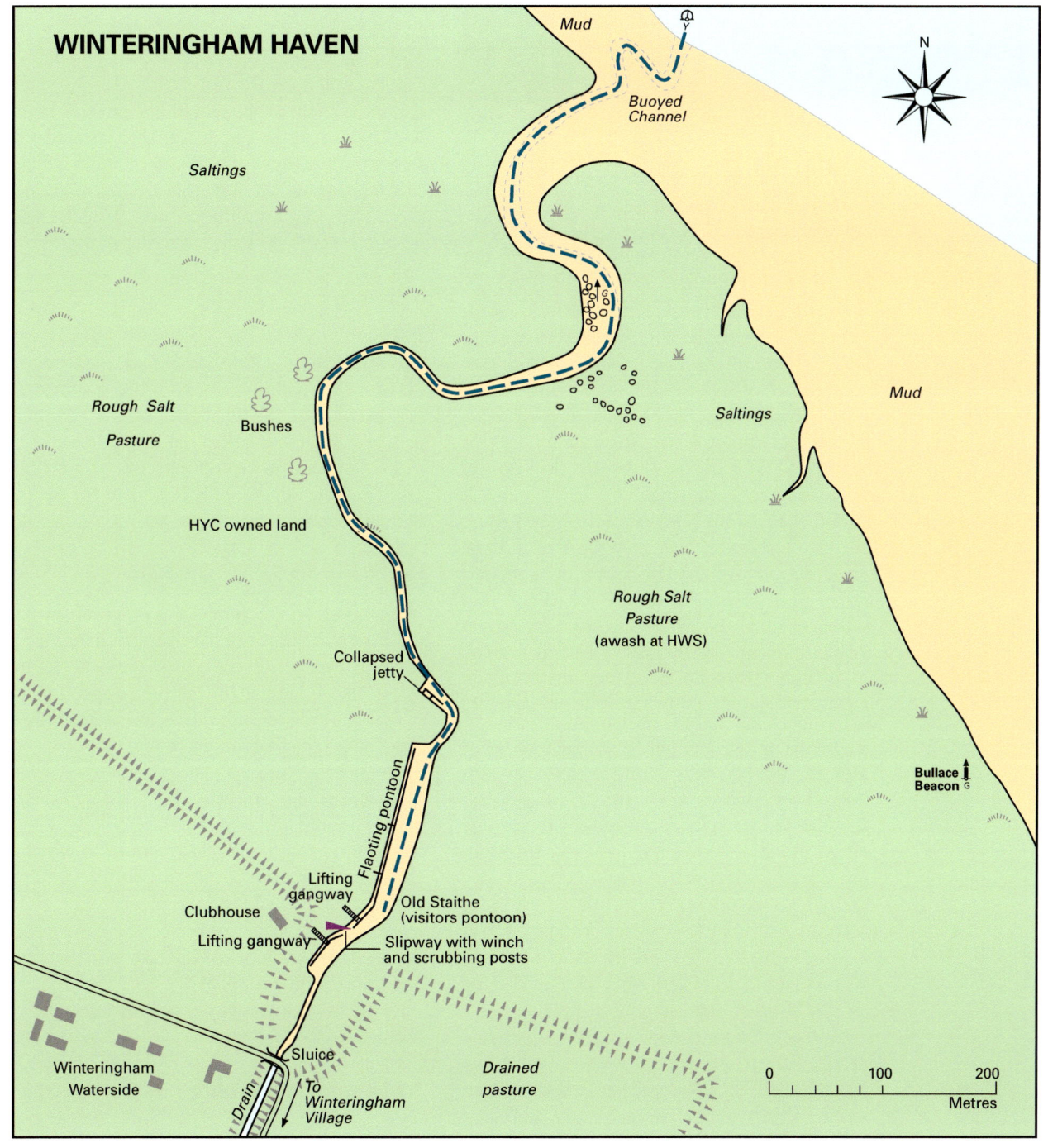

Hog's Back

Top: Hog's Back opposite Winteringham towards the north shore
David Wright

Bottom: Entrance to Winteringham at half tide
David Wright

a railway which fed the haven in its role as a port handling local cargoes.

Those days are gone, but the serpentine watercourse and tidal inlet remain and the enterprising Humber Yawl Club (HYC), founded in 1883 and with a clubhouse in Brough on the north shore, decided to acquire land which might suit their Lincolnshire members. Nothing more happened for some years, but in the late 1970s development began and today a thriving community of self-help, DIY enthusiasts have a club house, wooden stage moorings, a slipway and a varied programme of social and sailing events. They are also a RYA Recognised Teaching Establishment running a broad range of courses. All testament to the fact sailing need not be an elite, expensive pastime and can be enjoyed by many in many ways.

Approaches

All moorings dry and this needs to be factored into any plan to visit Winteringham. So too does the approach from the main, buoyed channel where in places charted drying heights are as much as 4m. There is a way through, however, which is monitored and marked by the HYC members. The club advise that according to tidal height and draught, access is approximately HW +/- 2h. But first-time visitors would do well to time their arrival for local HW when tidal set will be less.

A perpendicular drawn from the shore line at the haven entrance arrives around the No.33 SHM Fl.G.4s. less than 1M off. From this SHM mark, Winteringham church tower will bear approximately 215°, although it can be difficult to spot given the lie of the land. A useful transit includes wind turbines on the north shore and through SHM No. 33. Club advice however is to call ahead for the latest local knowledge of the channel and its changes. Take note that the buoyed channel in this vicinity is narrow and towards the Yorkshire north side a bank of mud; a hog's back has been growing steadily over recent years. Straying in this direction is not recommended.

At the time of writing, the Humber Yawl Club member in charge of moorings is contactable on ☏ +44 7581 176914 to give direction. The club house, not always open, can be called on ☏ +44 1742 733458. The channel, such as it is, winds between high banks covered in vegetation but as will be seen from the number and size of boats which call this home, the haven is perfectly viable given craft can take the ground. Which they do comfortably in soft, forgiving mud.

Moorings

A friendly innovation is the summer landing, a pontoon down creek which makes for easier berthing than the 'bows to' club moorings. No power or water here, but a simpler prospect with less risk of ending up aground in mid-stream with no chance of getting ashore. Consult the club's website for up to date information. www.humberyawlclub.com

Facilities and visitor information

The club and its members are welcoming and the usual facilities are here but not routinely, save for weekends during the season. Club boats also have use of a slipway and winch which could be available to temporary members, especially in extremis.

The nearby village, a short walk away, has the usual village amenity and The Bay Horse PH is friendly and comfortable. Noteworthy, is the Winteringham Fields restaurant which, along with the inn in nearby South Ferriby has Michelin Guide endorsement.
www.winteringhamfields.co.uk
Such establishments are relative rarities then two come along at once!

Less than a mile away is the Winteringham Haven Wildlife Reserve and for those seeking to stretch legs, the South Humber Heritage Trail is worth investigating. www.lincstrust.org.uk

Brough

More than a village, Brough is, these days, a prosperous settlement and still growing. The railway station makes for easy access to Hull and to the west, Doncaster and beyond. Some trains from Brough run to the more northern Yorkshire coastal towns.

In centuries past, Brough's claims to fame include being at the southern end of the Roman Cade's Road, which ran approximately northwards to what is now Newcastle upon Tyne. Later it had, amongst its residents, the highwayman Dick Turpin.

In recent, industrial times, BAE Systems (then British Aerospace) established a manufacturing facility here, where aircraft have been built and indeed flown since 1916. Sadly, this has now ceased, and at the last reckoning it was mooted the runway and airfield were to be built over.

Of most significance to the visiting sailor will be the Humber Yawl Club (HYC). Founded in 1883 and resident in Brough since 1919, it began at the instigation of Albert Strange and his compatriot George Holmes. Although Strange hailed from Gravesend in Kent, his contribution to sailing and yacht design was, during his time, much further north. Trained as an artist, he was headmaster of the Scarborough School of Art for 35 years and exhibited at the Royal Academy.

The Humber Yawl Club, which pioneered the use of sailing canoes with a yawl rig, now has over 300 members sailing yachts and various classes of dinghies. Essentially a club run by and for the benefit of its members, its home is firmly Brough through, since 1976, at Winteringham too on the south side of the estuary.

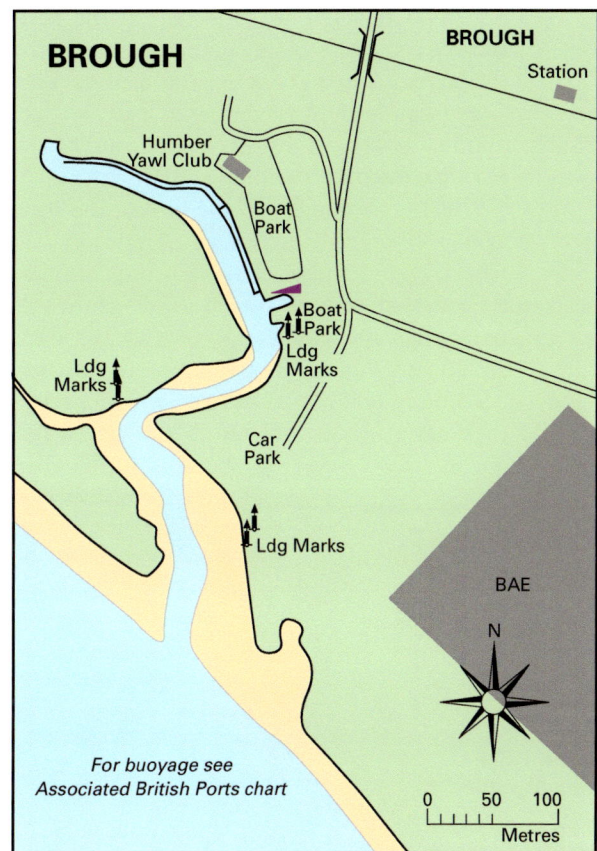

The BAE factory seen from the south shore but a clear visual reference to Brough Haven

Approaches and Entry

Brough Haven is drying and boats settle in soft mud. Moorings are stern or bow to with the opposite end secured to sunken moorings. Refer to ABP chart Barton Haven to Burton Stather which is updated bi-monthly. The club welcomes visitors but those who are unfamiliar with the channel should not rely on the precision of the fixed navigational marks, especially as the channel is not static. A sensible first step is to herald your intention to visit by calling the club in advance on ☏ +44 1482 667224. An enquiry of the club duty officer is also recommended.
northbankmate@humberyawlclub.com
www.humberyawlclub.com

Available water will depend on draught but vessels of no more than 1.5m can reasonably expect to enter from HW -2 hrs. A strong tidal set can occur across the haven entrance and first timers would do well to coincide arrival with local HW. Outer approaches will be from the main, Humber buoyed channel on a rising tide, from east of the haven, leaving the channel in the vicinity of SHM No.33

Fl.G.4s. Conspicuous from here is the BAE factory complex immediately downstream of the haven. When closer in, the Brough Tide Gauge can be seen towards the water's edge, and in the sailing season at least one of the HYC racing marks will be a useful reference.

When immediately off the haven, the rock armour flood wall (conspicuous) returns away from the river and gives an early indication of the entrance channel direction, which at this point runs approximately north/south. HYC set an outer mark in approximate position 53°43'·4N 000°35'·05W from which a series of leading marks indicate the deeper water route inward. Visitors are directed to moor near the mast hoist unless and until advised otherwise.

Facilities

The club has excellent facilities and affords the customary temporary membership to members of other clubs. It should be noted however that the clubhouse is not routinely open, hence the need to call ahead. The town has a good range of shops, two supermarkets, a medical centre, dentist, a post office and two pubs. And the railway station.

Pictured is *Sheila*, the oldest Albert Strange design known to survive. Built in 1905 for the artist Robert Groves and named after his daughter, 'Sheila', 25ft LOA came out of the yard of Robert Cain on the Isle of Man and is one of the finest, small vintage yachts still afloat. Once written off after a storm, she also suffered bomb damage in 1939 but continues to win trophies and is a tribute to Strange and his design ethos for boats to suit perfectly, the enthusiastic, small boat sailor *Jamie Clay*

Broomfleet

Simply that Broomfleet is there might well be an incentive for the more adventurous to include it in a Humber itinerary, and it is true that with the right, shallow draughted boat, an afternoon's creek crawling will reap its rewards. The village and its environs are, like many similar Humberside locations, an industrial archaeological treasure trove and the lock at the tidal end of the Market Weighton Canal is a structure of architectural importance.

Of possibly greater significance is off-lying Whitton Island, formed of the sands and gravels which accrete from river flow and which, over time, have been consolidated by vegetation. It now extends to some 120 hectares. Owned by Associated British Ports, the harbour authority, it is now leased to the RSPB who manage it as a nature reserve.

As a result of their activity, the island is now protected as a safe nesting habitat for avocet and provides feeding and roosting for pink footed geese, teal, wigeon, spoonbills, curlew and ringed plover.

Those afloat for leisure are increasingly aware of issues around the protection of wildlife and should not need reminding of the legislation which applies.

Broomfleet has a railway station on the Selby line.

Approaches and anchorage

A scoured channel between the island and the shoreline persists and is shown on the Barton Haven to Burton Stather chart. It can be >100m wide and have charted depths varying between 0.5m and 1.5m below chart datum. To either side, however, are drying heights of 2m plus. The canal lock structure is conspicuous, although not necessarily a reliable transit. The surest way of nosing in would be just after LW when more can be seen. An anchorage can be found nearer to the lock where depths are often greater. There is little by way of local amenity.

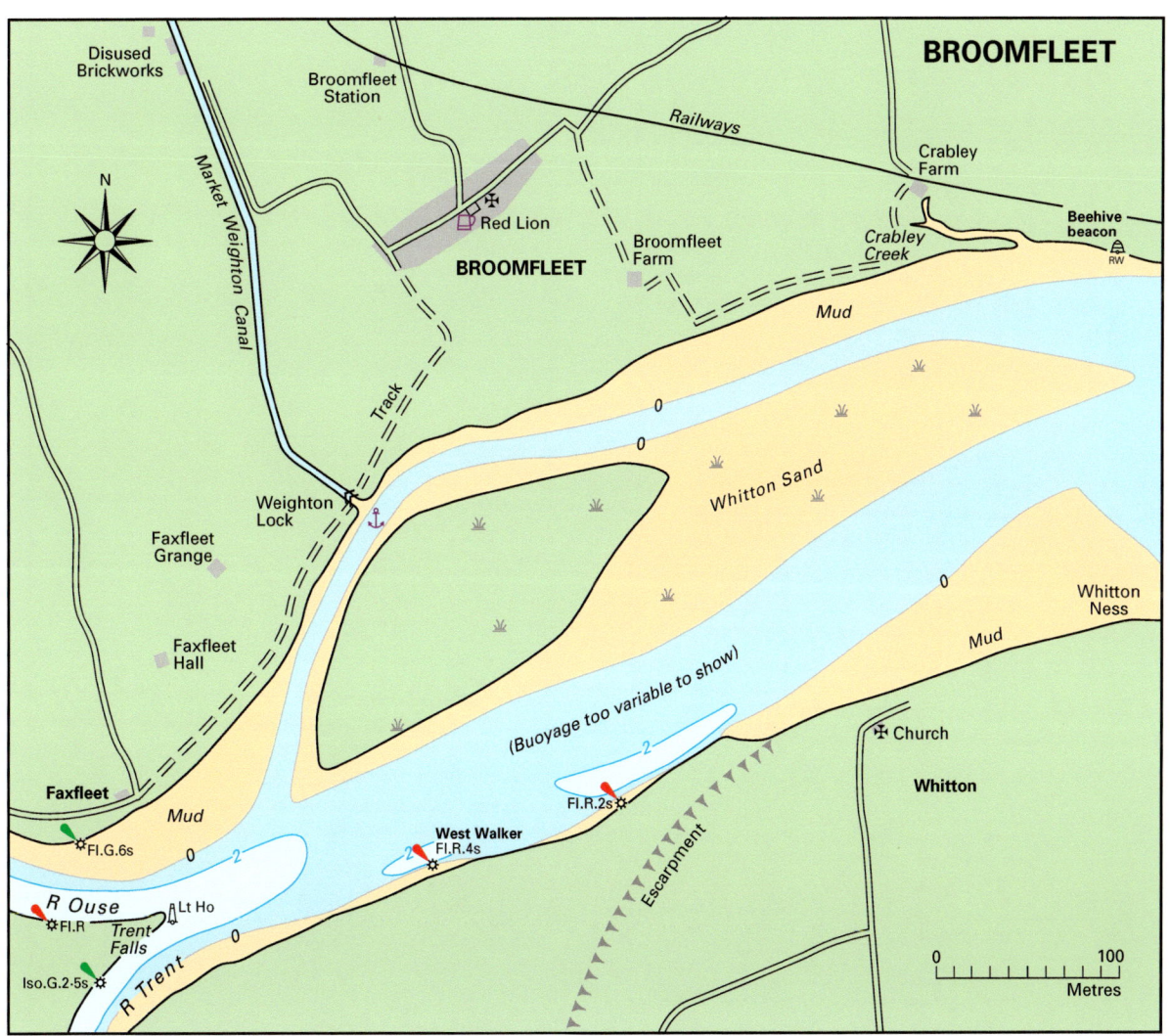

Norfolk, The Wash and Humber

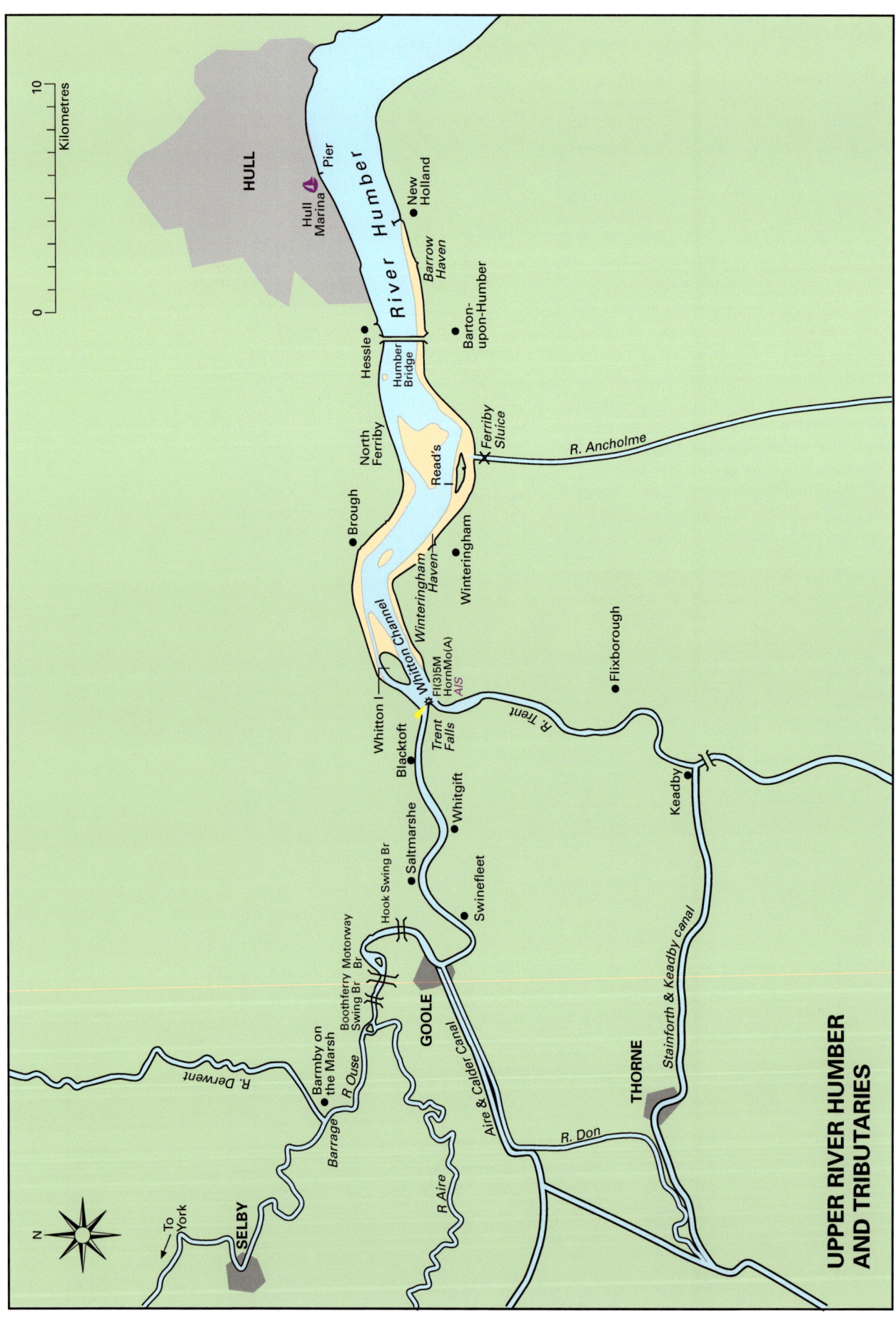

UPPER RIVER HUMBER AND TRIBUTARIES

Above Apex Light (Trent Falls)

⊕ 53°42'·02N 000°41'·50W.
White Sector 360°.

Apex Light is at the confluence of the Rivers Trent and Ouse which combine to form the River Humber. For those with suitable leisure craft, either motor yachts or those sailing with masts that can be lowered, it is not overstating the case that a season-long cruise can be enjoyed in these non-tidal waters. The British inland waterway network, accessed from the sea, compares favourably with all that continental Europe can offer, inland of its own sea ports.

The River Trent to Gainsborough

The Trent, the third-longest river in the UK, rises near Stoke and serves most of the central and northern midlands. It is navigable for nearly 120 miles and is tidal below Cromwell lock and weir in Nottinghamshire. Many canals branch off the river and leisure and commercial traffic is commonplace. On the tidal, lower reaches, vessels up to 100m LOA can be encountered. With the right boat you can cross the country via the connecting waterways and emerge in Liverpool, Bristol or London, enjoying everything in between.

For purposes of this pilot, basic coverage extends to the limit jurisdiction of the statutory harbour authority. For the River Trent that is Stone Bridge at Gainsborough, where the river remains tidal.

Charts

Associated British Ports: Barton Haven to Burton Stather. Burton Stather to Keadby. Keadby to Gainsborough. They can also be downloaded or viewed from the ABP Humber website where those displayed will reflect the latest surveys.
www.humber.com > Estuary information > Marine information > Chart Catalogue.

The Boating Association: Chart No.1 The Non-Tidal Trent. Chart No.2 The Tidal Trent.

VHF

Humber VHS 15 on the River Trent. VHF 17 for commercial wharves. VHF 74 for Canal & River Trust locks and bridges.

Bridges

Essential planning must take into account the physical constraints, in particular bridges on the lower reaches.

Keadby Bridge Air draught on MHWS 5.1m. An illuminated air draught gauge is downstream to the eastern bank close to the navigational arch.

M180 Motorway Bridge Air draught on MHWS 8.1m to the centre, 30m width.

Gainsborough Bridge Air draught on MHWS 4.7m

These bridges are marked with vertical red and green lights to the port and starboard hands respectively and a fixed yellow indicates arch centre.

Havens

Practicable mooring options out of the lower reaches of the river are:

1. Stainforth and Keadby Canal at Keadby (more accommodating); 7M upstream of Apex Light. Stainforth and Keadby: Lock restrictions. 18.8m LOA x 5.2m beam x 2.22m draught x 3.3m air draught.

2. Chesterfield Canal at Stockwith. This canal, known as Cuckoo's Dyke, is narrow. Chesterfield: Lock restrictions. 21.95m LOA x 2.08m beam x 0.98m draught x 2.15m air draught.

3. Gainsborough (21M upriver from Apex Light

More detailed information can be obtained of the non-tidal navigation authority, The Canal and River Trust.
www.canalrivertrust.org.uk
Keadby Lock ☎ +44 7733 124611

Anchorage

Less than 1M upstream from Apex Light, between South Trent Beacon and Addingfleet Drain Light, there is an anchorage towards the starboard (west) bank which can serve while waiting for a tide. It is clearly marked on the ABP chart. Charted depths of more than 4m. (See ABP chart *Barton Haven to Burton Stather*).

Pilotage upstream

For tides see page 60.

Enter the River Trent leaving Apex Light to starboard. Hold to the starboard bank close to the training wall until close to South Trent Beacon VQ G. The channel's deeper water is then to the port hand, using the Cliff End Beacons as a transit which are in line on 153°. This takes you east of Island Sand which dries at LW.

There are several shoals on the Lower Trent in addition to Island Sand. Mere Dyke, downstream of Flixborough, Keadby Bar, Derrythorpe and The Ewsters downstream of Owston Ferry. In the main, there are least depths of 1m over these shoals but this can reduce to 0.4m as conditions vary. There are tide gauges which give the level relative to chart datum at various locations.

Lit beacons to both banks, red to port and green to starboard, are found between Burton Stather and Keadby. Above Keadby, the channel changes with some frequency, so no directions can sensibly be given, unless of local provenance based on frequent passage making. Those visiting in small craft and wishing to carry the Trent to Gainsborough and beyond would do well to consult The Boating Association guides to the tidal and non-tidal river.

During spring tides, a tidal bore known locally as the Aegir can form on the first of the flood and reaches its peak between Owston ferry and Gainsborough about HW Hull – 1hr. It is greatest during equinoctial springs and is influenced in height and rate by fresh water volumes. The Environment Agency can advise in this respect.

Small craft can also be affected by drainage water pumped into the Trent upstream of Keadby Lock and from the River Idle at West Stockwith. A flashing yellow light is displayed when pumping takes place.

The River Ouse to Goole

One of several UK rivers so named, this Ouse runs for nearly 60 miles through Yorkshire and is a continuation of the River Ure. Together they form the sixth longest river in the UK. The Ouse has many tributaries which combine to drain a large part of the Pennines, Yorkshire Dales and North York Moors.

For the purposes of this pilot, there is the prospect of a passage upstream to York, which is eminently possible for motor vessels from seaward. Pilotage notes, however, are to Goole, above which The Boating Association chart provides the benefit of advice based on

---

Useful information – Goole (River Ouse)

Fairway buoy Key waymark is Apex Light, the confluence of the Rivers Trent and Ouse. 53°42'·02N 000°41'·48W.

Buoyed channel Humber Bridge to Apex Light approximately 10M. Well defined channel marked with buoys and light floats. Apex Light to Goole approximately 7.5M. Well defined river banks marked with beacons.

Moorings All afloat alongside moorings on Aire and Calder Canal. Goole Marina ☎ +44 1405 763985 Viking Marine ☎ +44 1405 765737. Check with marinas regarding draught as canal level varies. No air draught restrictions to this point.

Contacts ABP Contact via email or VTS on VHF. Ocean Lock Goole ☎ +44 1405 721128.
Harbour Authority ABP Humber.

VHF Port Working Channel Channel 15 in the sector above Humber Bridge. Inter-ship Channel 10.

Tidal predictions based on Hull (Albert Dock), Humber Bridge, Blacktoft, Goole. Goole difference on Hull (Albert Dock) approximately +1hr.

Inland waterways access Goole to Naburn Lock (sea lock) 27M. Thereafter non-tidal to York.

Hazards Commercial ship traffic to and from Goole. Give 24hr+ notice to Ocean Lock. Leisure craft should work on access from local HW -1/HW.

Note Passage planning outward to sea. It is possible if unable to lock out of Goole sufficiently before local HW that, depending on intended destination, there will be insufficient height of tide further downstream. An option is a passage anchorage near Apex Light, 1M inside the River Trent to await the next tide.

Charts Admiralty 3497 but for navigation above the Humber Bridge, the only charts showing soundings and buoyage are from Associated British Ports (ABP). Barton Haven to Burton Stather (updated bi-monthly) and Apex Light to Skelton Bridge (updated bi-annually). See www.humber.com

The River Ouse to Goole

local and frequent passage making and its coverage continues beyond the sea lock.

Commercial seagoing vessels use the river as far as Howden Dyke, just above the port of Goole. The river is tidal as far as Naburn where the locks can accommodate vessels up to 40.5m LOA and 7.6m beam. Indicated draught is 2.5m, varying from time to time according to river conditions. 24 hours' notice required ☏ +44 1904 728500. Apex Light to Goole is 7M. Goole to Naburn Lock is 27M. Naburn to York <5M.

Above Apex Light and for the length of the tidal river, there are no bank side small craft moorings save for in an emergency.

Charts

Associated British Ports: Upper Humber Barton Haven to Burton Stather. Apex Light (Trent Falls) to Skelton Bridge. Ouse Reaches. *Note* These charts are available in paper form from local agents. They can also be downloaded or viewed from the ABP Humber website where those displayed will reflect the latest surveys.

www.humber.com > Estuary information > Marine information > Chart Catalogue > Current Humber Charts.

The Boating Association Chart No.3. The Yorkshire Ouse. Tidal and Non-Tidal.

Imray *Map of the Inland Waterways of Great Britain. Inland Waterways of Great Britain.* Both titles by Jane Cumberlidge.

VHF

Humber VTS 15. Locks 74. Bridges VHF 09.

Bridges

Up to and including the port of Goole there are no height restrictions (Humber Bridge 29m MHWS).

Above Goole towards Naburn Lock and beginning with Skelton Railway Bridge, all bridges, with the exception of the M62 motorway bridge have the capacity to swing to allow vessels with greater air draught to pass.

Pilotage upstream to Goole

For tides see page 60.
Apex Light is a reporting point to VTS Humber from both directions. VHF 15.

If inward to Goole, arrange a lock opening giving as much advance notice as possible (at least 24h) to the Assistant Dock Master (ADM) at Ocean Lock on ☏ +44 1405 721128. VHF 14 is their working channel. Expect to be asked for vessel details, last port and number of souls on board, as well as ETA.

Enter the River Ouse passing Apex Light close to port at Trent Falls. Sail close to the training wall until you reach PHM No.2 Boundary East Ouse Beacon QR, from where the deeper water is to the starboard hand to Blacktoft Jetty. 53°42N 000°43W. Leading lights G. Rear occulting. Front flashing. This jetty, owned by Associated British Ports (ABP) is for the purpose of ship mooring in case of need, to await a tide inward or outward. Small craft are therefore discouraged from mooring here except in an emergency. In such a case, it is essential to advise VTS Humber on VHF 15 and/or the jetty on VHF 14. A mooring charge is levied.

The small craft alternative is to await a tide, either inward or outward at the anchorage in the River Trent, less than 1M upstream from Apex Light (see page 87).

Craft entering the Ouse can contact the Port of Goole or Blacktoft Jetty on VHF 14 for the latest information on water depth for various locations.

Above Blacktoft Jetty, lit beacons (red to port and green to starboard) mark each bank and act as leading lights in three reaches as the deeper water changes hand. Transits are as marked on the ABP chart *Apex Light to Skelton Bridge*.

The tidal Dutch River (lower River Don) enters the Ouse from the west bank immediately below Goole, downstream of the entrance to Ocean Lock. The south pier is lit FL.R 2.5s.

ABP advise lock opening as being HW − 3/+1.5 but leisure craft are recommended to

Goole inward, Ocean Lock
Mark Ashley Miller

Norfolk, The Wash and Humber

work to HW – 1/HW. In any case, a discussion with the Assistant Dock Master (ADM) as far in advance as possible is prudent as commercial ships arriving or leaving will likely be locking close to HW and small craft and ships are not locked through together.

ABP look to those crewing small craft to have at least one person on deck to handle mooring lines and, if possible, one forward and one aft. There are rescue ladders and wire strops running vertically in the lock chamber which can be used for securing temporarily.

Once through the lock, a turn to port brings the South Dock Bridge into view and the ADM will arrange a swing. Thereafter, a course through South Dock arrives at the Aire and Calder Navigation, readily identifiable by the many small vessels moored to both banks and in adjacent basins.

Goole

Goole presents a further Humber destination in its own right. A market town in the East Riding of Yorkshire, Goole is 19 miles directly south of York and 29 miles west of Hull. It is some 50M from the Spurn and 7M from Apex Light (Trent Falls). The enclosed docks date from 1826. There are Dutch connections too, the nearby River Don having been once diverted into the Ouse through the work of Cornelius Vermuyden. The lower Don becoming known as the Dutch River.

With an eight dock complex, commercial vessels up to 100m LOA and 4500 tonnes are routinely accommodated and a number of smaller, commercial vessels trade inland on the canal. An extensive range of marine trades is available nearby. From the point of view of the marine visitor, Goole represents secure and sheltered mooring and a convenient base from which to tour the region on land. It has all the amenity of a medium sized town within walking distance of the docks. There are good bus and railway links too.

Locking through into the Goole dock complex offers three mooring options at the beginning of the Aire and Calder Canal, after the swing bridge. First to port is Goole Marina, a 150 berth facility popular with narrow boats. There are alongside berths available in the canal stream. Marine trades and chandlery. ☎ +44 1405 763985. Immediately above here is a stretch of canal bank in the control of the adjacent auctioneers and valuers, Spicers. It is possible the moorings here benefit from a greater depth of water ☎ +44 1405 203203. Opposite Goole Marina is Viking Marine which also has a good range of services on hand. Contact Laird Cremer-Evans. ☎ +44 1405 765737.

Upstream of Goole

Navigation further upstream to York is best planned with the aid of The Boating Association chart/s and The Canal and River Trust publications.

The Aire and Calder Canal

The Aire and Calder canal continues to carry significant commercial traffic as well as being a popular route for suitable leisure craft, at least as far as Leeds, where the waterfront area has benefitted from considerable development of late: Cafés and bars; Leeds Art Gallery; The Royal Armouries Museum. There is much to interest the waterborne tourist.
www.visitleeds.co.uk/things-to-do/outdoors/leeds-waterfront

Leeds is also the junction with the Leeds and Liverpool Canal, a vital cross-Pennine link in the days of commercial canal traffic.

Alongside in Goole on the Aire and Calder canal *Mark Ashley Miller*

Above Goole there are no river moorings. The only practicable options are the non-tidal ones by locking through and into:

Selby Canal 14M above Goole. HW Hull +2/2.5h.

Naburn Lock 27M above Goole. HW Hull +3.5/4.5h.

As a general guide and based on the advice of The Boating Association, a motor cruiser should reach York from Apex Light in approximately seven hours.

York

York, founded by the Romans as Eboracum, grew over time as a major wool trading centre and became the northern ecclesiastical province of the Church of England. The large Gothic cathedral York Minster dominates the city.

Architecturally, York is largely unaltered and thus reflects its growth and development over centuries. Narrow, medieval streets abound. The centre is enclosed by the city's walls which are the most complete such defences in England, retaining all the principal gateways.

48 hour visitor moorings are available very near the railway station. There are marinas in the vicinity.

www.york.gov.uk/open-spaces/river-ouse/1

The navigation authority here is the Canal and River Trust.

www.canalrivertrust.org.uk/enjoy-the-waterways/canal-and-river-network/river-ouse

Pilotage downstream from Goole

For tides see page 60.

Leaving Goole seaward requires a deal of planning, not least over the preferred destination and its own tidal constraints.

Even a cursory study of the chart will reveal that to Apex Light (Trent Falls), the river is relatively narrow and natural scour achieves much in maintaining depth. Once east of Apex Light, however, the bathymetric picture changes radically as the banks recede and the estuary, in places, is almost 2M across. It was immediately upstream of the Humber Bridge where at least once, over an equinoctial spring low water, a local man with the advantage of being taller than average walked from bank to bank.

The corollary of this dire warning however is that commercial vessels, some loaded, leave Goole, and in due course the Humber, without coming to grief, so an uneventful passage is not beyond the ingenuity of anyone in command of a leisure vessel of relatively modest draught.

Canal traffic waiting for orders

Considerations will be time/speed/distance, preferred destination and alternatives in case of need. This in addition to when one's vessel can be locked out of Goole:

Available locking times vary according to source. ABP continue to advise HW -3hr/+1.5hr in their information for leisure craft users. The Boating Association give HW -2.5hr/+1.5hr, as do Admiralty Sailing Directions. But in late 2020, a breach of the canal bank at East Cowick resulted in significantly reduced locking availability because of the need for strict control of water levels. Over the ensuing period, ABP Goole were restricting lock operation to Local HW +/- 1hr. Even since the completion of repairs, these times remain the official availability. However, given that small craft leaving Goole with, for example, Hull Marina as an objective will almost certainly require earlier departure, local advice is to discuss requirements with the Assistant Dock Master at least 24 hrs before departure. A convenient arrangement should result.

ADM Goole ☎ +44 1405 721128.

Given an early locking out, part of an outward passage will be over foul tide and allowance needs to be made for reduced speed over the ground. Once beyond Apex Light, the benefit of the ebb will gradually kick in.

If needed, the anchorage within the River Trent, 1M from Apex Light is a good waiting option (see page 87).

Once in the Humber estuary, the buoyed channel is notable for its proximity to the south, Lincolnshire bank as it sweeps around the bight. (See photo page 79.) Thereafter and once through the Humber Bridge, choice of channel will depend on destination and be influenced by individual factors, not least the ever-changing depths reflected in the ABP charts which result from their regular surveys. If Hull bound then note well the ABP chart Hessle Sand.

# Index

Aire and Calder Canal 86, 90
Amy Howson 77, 79, 80
Ancholme, River 59, 77, 79
Ants, The 30, 48, 49
Apex Light 81, 86, 87-91
Associated British Ports (ABP) 6, 58, 59, 63, 69, 85, 89

Barrow-upon-Humber 1, 5, 72-74
Barton-upon-Humber 1, 5, 59, 74-76
Bays, The 10, 14, 27, 31, 34
Beacon Hill 14, 15
Black Sluice 52, 53
Blakeney 14, 16, 17-19
Blakeney Bar 18
Blakeney Harbour Association (BHA) 17
Blakeney Pit 5
Blakeney Quay 18
Blakeney Wreck Buoy 5
Boal Quay 38
Boating Association, The 6, 87, 88, 91
Boston 5, 12, 31, 47, 48, 51-53
Boston Deep 12, 30, 31, 47, 49, 55
Boston Gateway Marina 51, 53
Boston Stump 31, 49
Boston Tidal Barrier 51
bottled gas 45
Brancaster Bar 5
Brancaster Harbour 26
Brancaster Harbour Users Association 29
Brancaster Staithe 26-29
Brancaster Staithe Sailing Club 29
Brancaster Staithe Ski Boat Owners' Club 29
Bridgirdle shoal 10, 24
Brigg 77, 79
Broomfleet 85
Brough 1, 5, 82, 83-84, 86
Bulldog Channel 34, 35, 36, 37
Burcom Flats 5
Burcom Sand 63, 64
Burcom Shoal 64, 66
Burnham Deepdale 28
Burnham Flats Buoy 5, 8
Burnham Harbour Mouth 5
Burnham Norton 28
Burnham Overy Harbour 23-25
Burnham Overy Staithe 23, 25
Burnham Thorpe 23, 25

Cambridge 32, 34, 47
Canal and River Trust 90
charts 6, 59, 78, 87, 89
Chesterfield Canal 87
Clay Hole 31

Cley Harbour Project 19
Cley-next-the-Sea 14, 16, 18, 19
Coastal passages 9-13
Cork Hole 31
Crab Marsh Boatyard 44, 45
Cromer 1, 10, 12, 14, 15, 19, 23, 29
Cross Keys Marina 42-44
Cross Keys Swing Bridge 47

Daseley's Sled 31
Deep, The 70, 71
Delta 31
Denver Sluice 5
distances 5
Dog-in-a-Doublet Sluice 5, 40
Donna Nook Firing Range 11, 12, 60
Downs, The 14, 15
DZ buoys 11, 12, 32, 35, 40, 41, 48, 49

East Halton Skitter 67-68
East Lighthouse 32, 41, 43
Ely 32, 34, 47
Environment Agency 51, 53, 78, 79, 88

Fens Waterways Link 47, 52
Ferriby Sluice 5, 66, 77-80, 81, 86
Fisher Fleet 37
Fosdyke 5, 12, 47-50
Fosdyke Bridge 50
Fosdyke Yacht Haven (FYH) 49
Freeman Channel 12, 47

Gainsborough 87
Gat Channel 31
Gibraltar Point 31, 32, 49, 54
Gibraltar Point Nature Reserve 57
Gibraltar Point Sailing Club (GPSC) 12, 54, 57
Glandford Boat Club 77
Goole 5, 86, 88-91
Goole Marina 88, 90
Gore Middle 10, 27
Gore Point 15, 31
Grand Sluice 12, 47, 48, 51, 53
Grand Union Canal 40, 47
Great Ouse, River 12, 32, 34, 47
Grimsby 1, 5, 9, 10, 13, 59, 63-66, 74, 75, 76, 81, 86
Grimsby & Cleethorpes Yacht Club 63, 65
Grimsby Dock Tower 63
Grimsby Fish Dock 64
Grimsby Marina 64
Grimsby Royal Dock 65
Gun Hill 23, 24

Haile Sand Buoy 5
Haile Sand Fort (Tetney) 5, 61, 62
Hanseatic League 34, 38, 68
Harrison, John 72, 73, 74
Hedon 68
Hedon Haven 5, 68
Hessle 5, 59, 76
Holkham Bay 24, 31
Holkham Hall 19, 23
Holkham Meals 21
Hull 1, 5, 59, 68-72, 81, 83, 86, 88, 90, 91
Hull Marina 13, 58, 66, 70, 76, 86, 91
Hull Roads 69, 70
Humber Bridge 59, 60, 66, 70, 72, 74, 75, 78, 89, 91
Humber Cruising Association 63, 65
Humber Gateway Wind Farm 13
Humber Mouth Yacht Club 61
Humber Yawl Club (HYC) 82, 83
Humber, River 12, 59, 86, 87
Humber, The 1, 9, 12, 59-61
Hunstanton 14, 26, 29, 30, 31, 36

Immingham 58, 61, 64, 66, 67, 77
inland waterways 40, 59, 61, 85, 87, 89, 90, 91
Inner Dogs Head 30, 54
Inner Dowsing wind farm 8, 11, 12, 14
Inner Knock 49, 55

Kasbah, The 63
Keadby 5, 86
Lynn wind farm 11, 12, 30, 55
King's Lynn 12, 23, 24, 29, 31, 34-40

Lincoln 32, 47, 53, 66, 81
Lincolnshire Wildlife Trust 57
Louth 61
Louth Canal 61
Lower Harbour 18
Lower Road 31, 49
Lowestoft 1, 9, 10, 40
Lynn 5, *see also King's Lynn*
Lynn Knock 12
Lynn Pilots 36

Manchester 66
Maritime Safety Information (MSI) broadcasts 2
Market Weighton Canal 85
Middle Bank 10, 27, 30
Middle Level 47
Morston Quay 16, 18, 19
Mow Creek 26, 28

92

Index

National Coastwatch Institution 2
National Nature Reserve (Scolt Head Island) 29
Nelson, Horatio 23, 25, 40
Nene, River 9, 12, 32, 40-41, 42
New Holland 5, 72, 86
Norfolk Coastal Path 15, 19, 26
North Killingholme 5
North Norfolk 9, 15
Northampton 40, 47
Norton Creek 26, 27, 28

Ocean Lock 88, 89
Old Hunstanton 30, 31, 36
Ouse Amateur Sailing Club 39, 40
Ouse, River 59, 81, 88-90
Outer Dogs Head 12, 30, 31, 49, 54, 55
Outer Westmark Knock 31, 40
Overy Staithe 23-25

Parlour Channel 55
Paull 68, 70
Peddars Way 15
Peterborough 32, 40, 46, 47
Purfleet 39

Read's Island 78, 79
Roaring Middle 11, 14, 30, 34, 35, 47, 48
Rolling Roads diagrams 9-13
Ropewalk gallery 76
Royal Dock 63

Sail The Wash vi, 38, 55
Saltfleet 5, 11, 61
Sandringham House 40
Scolt Head Island 15, 23, 24, 25, 26
Scullridge 48, 49
Sheringham Shoal wind farm 17, 22
Skegness 30, 57
Skitter Channel 73
Skitter Haven 67-68
South Ferriby 66, 77-80, 82
South Ferriby Marina 79, 80
South Forty Foot Drain 52
South Quay 39
South Sunk Sand 31
Spalding 47, 50
Spurn Head 1, 11, 13, 60
Stainforth and Keadby Canal 86, 87
Stamford 47
Standard House Chandlery 23
Stiffkey 16, 18, 19
Stone Creek 66
Storm surges 2
Strange, Albert 83, 84

Sunk Island 66
Sutton Bridge 5, 12, 31, 40-44, 45, 47
St Botolphs *see Boston Stump*

Tabs Head 12, 47, 49, 51
Tetney 5, 60, 61-63
Thornham 14, 29
Thornham coal barn 29
tidal streams 3
tide gauge(s) 21, 41, 47, 60, 64, 78, 84, 88
tides 3, 60
Trent Falls 5, 86, 87-91
Trent, River 59, 81, 86, 87-88, 89, 91
Trial Bank 30, 31, 41

Vancouver 39
Viking Way 76

Wainfleet former firing practice area 48, 49, 55
Wainfleet Haven 5, 12, 49, 54-57
Wash, The 9, 12, 31-34
Waters' Edge Visitor Centre 75, 76
weather 2
Welland, River 12, 32, 47, 49, 50
Wells Fairway Buoy 5
Wells Quay 5
Wells-next-the-Sea 9, 14, 15, 17, 20-23, 24, 26, 29
Whitby 9
Whitton Island 85
wind farms iv, 8, 13, 55
winds 2
Winteringham Haven 81-82, 86
Wisbech 5, 10, 12, 31, 35, 40-41, 44-47
Wisbech Yacht Harbour 42, 45
Witham, River 12, 32, 47, 52
York 59, 76, 90